THE
CAKE
COOK
BOOK

HANNAH GRANT

THE CAKE COOKBOOK

Copyright © Hannah Grant™ and HGC ApS 2022
Hannah Grant™ is a registered Trademark
Musette Publishing CPH ApS
www.hannahgrant.com

M[U]SETTE
PUBLISHING

Photographs © Hannah Grant
Dr. Stacy Sims portrait © Stacy Sims
Art Direction & Design: HGC Design / Strong Point
Editor: Musette Publishing CPH
Proofreading: proofed.com
Copy-editing: Various artists

Print and publishing partner:
Helmin & Sorgenfri
https://www.helminsorgenfri.dk

Helmin & Sorgenfri

THE
CAKE
COOK
BOOK

Printed by P&B Print
1st edition. 1 impression, printed in Latvia
ISBN 978-87-94190-16-9

Other Cookbooks by Hannah Grant:

The Grand Tour Cookbook
(Danish 2013, Czech 2014, English, German, French 2015)
English: ISBN 978-87-998169-0-3

Eat Race Win – The endurance athletes cookbook
(English 2018, Czech 2021)
English: ISBN 978-87-998169-1-0

For upcoming events and more information, please go to:
www.hannahgrant.com
Social media:
Instagram @dailystews
Facebook @hannahgrantcooking

Scan to visit Hannahgrant.com

THIS BOOK BELONGS TO:

_____

EAT YOUR CAKE AND YOUR VEG

HAVE
GIES TOO

TABLE OF CONTENTS:

HANNAH'S MISSION

"Teaching people to bake, cook and be creative in the kitchen, through healthy cooking with everyday ingredients, whilst growing their kitchen self-esteem through online engagement and delicious, fun and simple recipes."

The Cake Cookbook Manifesto

1.   Eat cake with a good conscience

2.   Always share your cake

3.   Build a community of fellow minded cake lovers

4.   Spread the word of healthy baking

5.   Use limitations to spark creativity

6.   Never compromise flavor

7.   Push boundaries for what is seen as cake

8.   Challenge the doubters

9.   Bake the change

INTRODUCTION

Dear Reader,

If you're reading this, there's a good chance that you are someone who wants to live a healthy lifestyle, but also loves to eat cake. You might be an aspiring or very serious endurance athlete or possibly all of the above. Either way, you're in the right place.

For the past decade, I have cooked for some of the world's best pro cyclists and have developed recipes for very serious competing endurance athletes to help them optimize their performance. Over the years, I have attempted to bake "healthy" cakes without heaps of added sugar or the use of wheat flour and dairy, without compromising the results. To be completely honest and transparent with you, these cakes didn't always turn out the way I had imagined, and the pro riders on the cycling team weren't very happy when I compromised the original recipes too much. Nevertheless, when we experience failure, we can learn from it and become smarter, faster, and better.

This book is my mission to make a change and the result of testing hundreds of ways to bake delicious cakes that don't screw up your gut, and that make you feel great during training, racing, and parties. Yep, you read that right; these cake recipes are great for training and racing AND you can serve them at your kid's birthday party, or when your friends and family come around for dinner. The recipes in this book have been tested by thousands of athletes, their kids, and their families, and they all love these easy-to-make recipes.

So, what is so special about my cake recipes?

As the Cake Cookbook manifesto states, limitation sparks creativity. That's why all my recipes are gluten- and dairy-free; most of them are made without added sugars and are packed with vegetables. A lot of the recipes use sweet potato and potato as the base, instead of wheat flour. Root vegetables, such as carrots, beets, and sweet potatoes have a natural sweetness to them, especially when they are cooked, making the cakes rich in flavor and complex in sweetness. These vegetables are also packed with vitamins and dietary fibers, aiding a well-functioning digestion, gut and healthy body. One section of the book highlights recipes that use alternative flour types for delicious and elaborate gluten-free, dairy-free, and vegan cakes, most of them without added sugars, making it easy to bake mouthwatering cakes that suit your dietary needs.

The best thing about these recipes is: You can have your cake and eat your veggies too!

What's not to like?

Now, let's bake a change.

– Hannah

"A PARTY
A CAKE IS
MEETING!

-JU

WITHOUT
JUST A
LIA CHILD

A Cake Dilemma and a Pandemic Later

Have your cake and eat your veggies too

Baking a cake is easy; all you need is sugar, butter, eggs, and flour.
This book could easily end right there if it was a normal baking book, but that would be the most boring book on the planet, full of recipes you've already seen floating around on the internet from an abundance of food bloggers.
There's no need for me to copy and paste boring ass recipes to reprint them here.

This book is for those who want to think outside the box. It's a new way of thinking about cake, so you can have your cake and eat your veggies too.

It all starts with cake

My relationship with cake stems from decades of frustration and gender stigma around the sweet treat. I've had a very ambivalent relationship with making and baking cakes, and for years, I did everything I could to avoid it. But the truth of the matter is: everyone loves cake, and you can't run away from it, especially not if you want to be liked and have people give your recipes a try.
It all starts with cake, whether you like it or not.

I've always been frustrated with the cake and dessert stigma that sticks to women.
Cakes, fluffy frosting, white flour, and pure sugar. Housewife vibes from the 1950s combined with nursing, caring, and being ever so sweet and happy. Girls in pink dresses with princess tiaras, raised to understand that being sweet and beautiful is the way to succeed in life to find a man that will provide for them and their kids, all while they live happily ever after in a Xanax haze.
In my eyes, all of this could be compressed into a screamingly sweet pink cupcake with cream cheese and butter icing sprinkled with glitter confetti. Something that looks so innocent, yet still holds the patronizing gender stigma. It's even been transferred to marketing and businesses pink it and shrink it.

The early years

As a chef apprentice, I saw the split of the genders in the kitchens. A very old-school understanding and way to divide the chefs, the men would cook steaks and make everything salty, and the women would make delicate things, such as dessert, pastries, and appetizers. Sweet and feminine edibles were a woman's job, and that seriously provoked me.

In 2003, to fit in while working in kitchens as a woman, you would have to act like a man, speak like a man, and be tougher than your male peers to get to the "real cooking" at the meat station. Otherwise, you would be relegated to staying back in the sweet kitchen. The sweet kitchen was strictly recipe based, and if you tried to freestyle a recipe, the chances were that it wouldn't work out. There was no room for creative freedom in making ice creams, sorbets, chocolate fondants, or crème brulées other than the flavor, and which mousse, fruit, or tuille to serve next to it. To me, the sweet kitchen was a sugary, awful hell hole that everyone adored from the outside. Let me tell you, I did not want to be put in there.

PRO CYCLING: SPECIAL DIETS

When I started working with the pro cycling team, they always requested cake. It's no surprise that cyclists love cake, and the soigneurs would ask me to bake giant cakes for them to cut and pack for their musette bags every day. I was new to the team and was hired to change the diet for the riders, cutting down on processed foods. The best way to do this was to minimize wheat, dairy, and refined sugar in their daily meals because their sugar intake was already very high from eating gels and
synthetic energy bars at the races.

Baking cakes was not the problem. Baking cakes without wheat flour, dairy, and too much sugar, now that was tricky; especially if the point of the cake was to get the riders to eat it.
I started exploring gluten-free cakes in an abundance of variations. One cake at a time, I learned what worked and what didn't work. Success was based on the following reactions from the riders:

1. Eating the cake
2. Eating the cake and not complaining
3. Asking for more cake
4. Not commenting on weird texture or a lack of something
5. Wanting to build a factory to produce that type of cake in abundance

Slowly my experiments turned into something that was an interesting game to win, and baking cakes without "normal" cake ingredients became a dogma I lived by.

After hundreds of cake versions, a pandemic, and an army of amazing athletes around the world testing my recipes, I have now conquered my cake vendetta. My victory resulted in an abundance of cake recipes that are not like other cakes, with bases made from vegetables, that prove you can have your cake and eat your veggies too.

This book is my mission to bake a change, changing the status quo of cake baking. Thanks for joining the tastiest cake baking revolution.

ABOUT HANNAH

I was born in Denmark in 1982 to a Danish mother and a Scottish father. Growing up in a loving and creative family filled with people from the theater and restaurant industries, my unique background has fired my passion for food, creativity and cooking, which have been my life's work.

After a year spent in the Danish Royal Navy in 2003, I joined a culinary institute in Copenhagen to pursue my dream of combining creative skills and cooking with traveling, all the while continuing to learn, evolve, and develop.

Diploma in hand, I then ventured into some of the best restaurants in the world, including the Fat Duck in the U.K. and Noma in Denmark, before the door of opportunity opened to a completely different world of food and endurance sport.

I first spent a year on a kiteboarding expedition boat sailing the South Pacific, where I sourced local ingredients and cooked wholesome meals for the kiteboarders and surfers on board. It was an experience that triggered a new and exciting interest in nutrition, special diets, and performance fuel – the start of a unique culinary adventure that would shape my life more than I ever imagined.

In 2010, I was hired by Bjarne Riis to cook for the riders on his professional cycling team Saxo Bank. Throughout the season, I traveled full-time with the team through the incredible culinary touchpoints of France, Italy, and Spain.

Based on my work with the cycling team, I created the, now classic cycling must-have cookbook, The Grand Tour Cookbook. It was originally published in Danish and was then translated into English, Czech, French, and German in 2015. In 2016, it ended up in the hands of an American TV producer, who took the core themes of the book and translated it into the TV show "Eat. Race. Win." (available on Amazon Prime), which followed me and my crew as we cooked for a cycling team throughout the 2017 Tour de France. The show was nominated for two Emmy Awards and took one statuette home.

During my time with the cycling team, I developed a close working relationship with sports physiologist Dr. Stacy Sims, Ph.D. We have since started bringing innovative ideas to the table about fueling endurance athletes at the highest level. It was the start of the process that would end with the publication of The Endurance Athlete's Cookbook, Eat Race Win, in 2018. One thing led to another, and we started working on hydration and sleep products together, venturing outside of endurance sports, to cater to anyone who wants to live a healthy, active life style, staying sharp in the mind and body and optimizing sleep and hydration levels to be the best version of themselves at home, at work and anywhere else. You can get more info on these endeavors at hannahgrant.com.

My culinary experiences in the world of high-performance food have taken me around the globe and today, I write cookbooks, cook on TV, develop recipes making sure that people are well hydrated and sleeping better than ever. Today, I live and work in Copenhagen, so if you're in town you might bump in to me.

Thanks for reading,

Enjoy the cake, Hannah

Follow my adventures on **hannahgrant.com**

FOLLOW ME HERE

 @hannahgrantcooking

 @dailystews

HOW TO USE MY RECIPES

DIETARY PREFERENCES AND RECIPE SYMBOLS

To make it very easy for you, all recipes have symbols indicating what dietary preferences fit which cakes and if they are gluten free, dairy free, have no added sugar or if they are vegan.

(G)   **Gluten Free**

(D)   **Dairy Free**

(S)   **No added sugar**

(V)   **Vegan**

Why Gluten-free?

In my opinion, the world just needs more alternatives to baking with wheat flour. Over the years I've had so many happy messages from celiac people and those who have decided to live without gluten for personal reasons, telling me they can finally make delicious gluten-free cakes that the whole family wants to eat.

No Dairy?

Yes! Back in 2013, I spent a full month working with the cycling team at the Giro in Italy, drinking Cappuccinos daily like it was nobody's business. On an especially hot day, I could feel that something was wrong, and to my surprise, I discovered I can't tolerate dairy in my diet, I probably never could. I'll spare you the gory details. As a chef, I thought my culinary creative life had ended, until I realized that with limitations comes creativity, and from that day on, I saw my intolerance as a fun puzzle to solve, developing recipes without instead of recipes with.

No Added Sugars?

In most things processed and baked, you will find an abundance of added sugars.

Added sugars are sugars that don't occur naturally in the whole ingredients used, such as dried fruits, fresh fruits, and root vegetables. Added sugars can come in many versions, the most common ones being refined sugar, invert sugar, and high fructose corn syrup. Typically, the added sugars only add calories to your diet and have no essential nutrient content. They are added to a product or recipe to enhance the sweetness, texture, and flavor, as well as extend its shelf life. But these refined, processed sugars are not the only ones; honey and maple syrup fall into the category as well. Even though they are natural ingredients, these sweet liquids hold no dietary fiber and will still spike your blood sugar.

If you are trying to live a healthy lifestyle without added sugars, it can be quite tricky to find cake recipes that accommodate this without being packed with artificial sweeteners or just being a bad, dry, boring cake recipe. (Don't get me started on the artificial sweeteners. Hint: You can read more about these on pages 40-41 in Eat Race Win.)

Vegan Cakes?

Indeed! During the pandemic, when I was developing recipes and sharing them with thousands of people, I often got requests for vegan cakes or was asked if my recipes could be made without eggs. Honestly, this wasn't something I had given much thought to, but just as with the dairy dogma, I took the without as a challenge and started testing a lot of vegan cake recipes. It was an interesting and difficult experience; most of the recipes I found had a lot of sugar in them and used wheat flour. Suddenly, it wasn't only a single without, but a whole bundle of them I had to juggle. On top of that, a lot of them were just bad cakes and recipes. But through trial and error and a lot of patience, I developed an excellent selection of vegan cake recipes that don't use wheat or refined sugar and don't come out dry and awful. Try them for yourself.

Common Sense

When following my recipes, it is important to always use common sense. For example, you should keep in mind that the density, texture, and water content of different vegetables and fruits change throughout the year, and this can affect baking times. It's always important to keep an eye on the cake as it bakes, no matter what a recipe says, as some ingredients cook faster than others.

Every oven is different. If you cook frequently and are familiar with the proclivities of your oven, perhaps yours gets hotter in the upper right-hand corner, please take this into account. Your oven might be more powerful than mine, or it might cook more evenly. As a result, your dish might be done a little bit before the recipe dictates.

Personally, I always make notes in my cookbooks after I follow a recipe so that I know exactly how to make it perfect in the future.

The Notebook

If you have Eat Race Win, the cookbook, or follow me on Instagram (dailystews), you know I love notebooks and always transfer my chosen recipe from any cookbook to my recipe notebook. I have done this since I was an apprentice, and it has taught me several things:

- ◼ It ensures I know all the steps I will need to take.

- ◼ It ensures that I have all the ingredients ready to make the cake.

- ◼ It allows me to write detailed notes next to the recipe, so I remember what I subbed and if a recipe needed a longer baking time or fewer berries.

I don't like to write in printed recipe books; I like to keep them as pure as possible. I'm not a dog ear kind of girl either. All my notebook recipes are dated, and I always note the occasion for the recipe I've written. If I go back and use the same recipe again, it's a fun way to keep memories of good times and great recipes.

Over the years, you will have notebooks full of your favorite recipes from all your cookbooks at home, making them easy to bring along if you, like me, love to cook and bake when you travel for work or vacation.

As a chef this becomes a little recipe diary, you can see here what my notebook (that I still use) looks like.

My notebook - which I started in 2014 - still going strong

Adjust The Portion Sizes

The recipes can be baked either as one large cake, two smaller ones, or as portion-sized muffins. The muffins are very easy to pack and bring along for rides, races, picnics, lunches, and events.

If you decide to bake the recipe as portion-sized muffins, please note that the baking time will be about 25-40% less than if you were baking a full-sized cake. A good pointer: Muffins tend to bake in 25-30 minutes.

Portion sized cakes

Full size cake

Nutrition Facts: Scan the QR Code for Macros

If you need to get the macros for any of the cake recipes, you can scan the QR code on this page to get the info. Alternatively, you can go to hannahgrant.com and find it all there.

NOTE:
If you adjust or replace ingredients, the nutritional content will change.
If you decrease coconut oil in a recipe, you must be aware that the taste and texture will also change, the same applies if you change the amount of dates, maple syrup or honey.

Make It Easier: Bake Plenty

While you're at it, you might as well double up the recipe and bake enough for your freezer.
All cake recipes are suitable to keep frozen for up to three months.

Machine or Human Power

If you don't have a food processor at home, you can still make the vegetable recipes. However, they will be a little bit chunkier.

To make the raw veg cakes without a food processor or blender, you will need a shredder, and a bit of patience, for chopping dates as finely as possible.

If you only have a stick blender, you can use that to blend chopped dates, eggs, and liquids before you fold them into the batter. However, do note that once you get a food processor, your life will change drastically. If you don't want to pay for a brand new one, you can find great used ones online for very little money. Make sure to choose one that has more than 700 watts, preferably 1000 or more, as these machines can run for longer at a time without overheating. Also a food processor will make general meal prep so much easier.

Greasing and Dusting vs. Baking Paper

Depending on what type of baking tin you're using and the state of it, you can go for two options here.
In most kitchens, you will find a stack of older and newer cake tins; some might be rusty, some the non-stick coating is flaking off, and some could be in mint condition. Once you have assessed the state of your equipment, you will choose your method to prevent your cakes from sticking.
Here is a general rule:
Beaten up cake tins: Baking or parchment paper
Mint condition: Grease and dust

1. The Grease and Dust Method
    Grease up the baking tin with a teaspoon of coconut oil or a lump of butter (plant-based or regular), use a paper towel to hold the lump, and make sure to spread it out evenly, getting it into all the little edges and corners. Next, throw a handful of oat flour or a nut meal of your choice into the tin and rotate the tin around until all surfaces are covered. If there is any excess dust left, make sure to tap it out of the tin.

2. Baking or Parchment Paper
    Shape the baking paper to fit the cake tin. I personally grease the baking paper with a bit of oil to avoid the cake sticking to the paper after baking.

SUBSTITUTES AND SEASONALITY

Seasonality

When you are baking, the best results always come from using ingredients that are in season, when flavors and textures are at their peak, prices are good, the stock is plentiful, and the flavors are sweet and delicious.

I designed all the recipes in this book to be flexible, with an eye toward the availability of ingredients, where you can easily substitute one type of vegetable for another that is similar or swap nuts and seeds as you please. I invite you to play around with flavors and create your own personal versions of my cakes.

Many of the cakes have fresh fruit in them, here any type of berry or fruit can typically be substituted with another that has similar texture and density. This means swapping raspberries for blackberries, and not rock-solid unripe pears. As you can imagine, the last substitution will likely not end up very delicious, with an undercooked pear and an over-baked cake.

Oats and wheat substitutes

Oats are naturally gluten-free, but they are often processed at plants that handle products that contain gluten. Therefore, if you are celiac, you should always choose oats labeled specifically with a gluten-free label. This ensures that they have been processed in a clean plant with no cross-contamination.

Most of my recipes use oats as a dry ingredient base, but if you want to substitute the oats, you have a few options. Keep in mind that what you choose will affect the texture and flavor of the finished result.

For baked cakes, you can use quinoa flakes, gluten-free flour mix, fine cornmeal, or tapioca flour (not corn starch). If you have no issues with gluten, you can simply use wheat flour. You can even use a plant based protein powder.

Potato Starch vs. Corn Starch

When you bake with different types of starch, it's important to understand how to use them when baking to avoid a mealy or floury feeling in your mouth from the raw starch.

The vegan recipes I have developed use a mixture of potato starch and corn starch that, if not baked long enough, will leave you with a very unsatisfying result. Therefore, the baking times are longer, and the liquid content in the recipes is higher.

Using Chocolate

If you decide to throw in a handful of chocolate chips or chunks in a recipe, please note that, depending on what chocolate you use, it might contain traces of milk. Pay close attention to the packaging to make sure it specifically says vegan or dairy-free. If a recipe is marked as vegan and you decide to go for milk chocolate, it will no longer be vegan.

Also, beware of the sugar content in the chocolate; if you are trying to avoid added sugars, go for at least 70% dark chocolate.

SUBSTITUTES

Nuts and Seeds

If you keep the ratios the same in the recipes, any nut or seed can be substituted with another one of your choosing. Keep in mind that the flavor of the cake will change depending on what you choose to use. Flax seeds are not a good substitute for other seeds due to their ability to become extremely sticky. These are, however, great as egg substitutes. More on that later.

Most of the recipes have almonds as the main nut because they have a very neutral and mild flavor, but feel free to play around and mix and match as you please.

- Hazelnuts
- Walnuts
- Pecans
- Pistachios
- Brazil nuts

- Cashews
- Sunflower seeds
- Pumpkin seeds
- Sesame seeds
- And more...

Egg Substitutes

There is a vegan way to substitute an egg. It's a simple swap, but you might find that the cake can become a little denser and fall apart more easily.
The flax egg will not work in the recipes with baked sweet potato, such as the rhubarb cake, but should work great in all the other recipes.

How to make flax egg
1 egg = 1 Tbsp. ground flax or chia seeds + 2.5 Tbsp. water.
Combine well and let sit for five minutes before using it.

Butter, Fats, and Oils

Coconut oil can be substituted for regular butter or plant-based "butter."

Neutral tasting oils can be substituted with milder tasting oils; just be aware that the flavor of the oil will affect the finished result.

Personally, I use either neutral-tasting coconut oil or a good quality plant-based "butter." The market for this type of product has really boomed, and there are actually some great-tasting versions out there, if you ask me.
I know all my old chef colleagues will not agree with me; in their eyes, nothing beats butter from a cow. But in the end, you decide; the recipes will work with either.

However, the only products I don't recommend using are cheap kinds of margarine and palm oil.

BAKING TEMPERATURES & TIMES

Different Ovens

All ovens seem to have their own baking personality. If you use your oven regularly, you will know that it might overbake things in the bottom left corner or the center to the right. You need to consider your oven's specific conditions when baking.

Rotating the pan once or twice while baking can be beneficial. Keep an eye on your cake while it's baking to make sure you get an even bake.

Convection vs. regular

A hot air oven circulates the heat and should bake more evenly than a regular oven. All my cakes have been baked in a conventional home oven with hot air. If you are baking the cakes in a regular oven, you might need to adjust the temperature up about 15°C/20°F and possibly extend the baking time by a few minutes.

Lower Temperatures

The recipes baked at lower temperatures typically contain potato, corn starch, or another type of flour or grain that needs a longer baking time to avoid having that dry and mealy feeling in your mouth when you eat the cake. These recipes also have more liquid in them to prevent them from drying out during the extended baking time. With a lower temperature for a longer period, the cakes will turn golden brown and initially have a thicker crust. As the cake cools and sits in the fridge, it will even out the moisture and make the whole cake nice and soft. With that said, you can totally eat the cakes without letting them sit in the fridge for hours or overnight.

Higher Temperatures

Baking at higher temperatures makes the cake set and brown faster. It also makes the eggs in the recipe soufflé and aids in making the cake less dense.
Pay close attention to a cake that is baked at higher temperatures; even a few minutes too long can mean the end to an otherwise delicious recipe. Always keep an eye on the oven, and don't just blindly trust that the recipe and your oven are a match made in heaven.

Short vs. long baking time

It might be obvious, but the shorter the baking time, the softer and possibly more under-cooked the cake will be, and the longer the baking time, the firmer and more cooked it will be. For cakes made of raw vegetables, the baking time will be a lot longer, giving the vegetable time to fully cook and develop a nice, aromatic, sweet flavor.
When baking any of the recipes from this book, if you find that one of the cakes was a little too dry or maybe a little too wet, simply jot it down in your notebook. Next time, you will know that the cake needs to be baked a little more or a little less.

CONVERSION TABLE

Milliliters (mL) to Cups (C)

Multiply milliliters with 0.004227
E.g. 400 mL * 0.004227 = 1,69 C

Milliliters	Cups
1	0.0042
50	0.21
100	0.42
125	0.53
150	0.63
200	0.85
250	1.06
300	1.27
350	1.48
400	1.69
450	1.90
500	2.11
600	2.54
700	2.96
800	3.38
900	3.80
1000	4.227

Grams (g) to dry Ounces (oz.)

Multiply grams with 0.0353
E.g. 200 g * 0.0353 = 7,06 oz.

Grams	Ounces
1	0.035
50	1.77
75	2.65
100	3.53
125	4.41
150	5.30
175	6.18
200	7.06
250	8.83
300	10.59
400	14.12
500	17.65
600	21.18
700	24.71
800	28.24
900	31.77
1000	35.3

Grams (g) to Pounds (lb.)

Multiply grams with 0.0022
E.g. 800 g * 0.0022 = 1,76 lb.

Grams	Pounds
1	0.0022
50	0.11
75	0.165
100	0.22
125	0.275
150	0.33
175	0.385
200	0.44
250	0.55
300	0.66
400	0.88
500	1.1
600	1.32
700	1.54
800	1.76
900	1.98
1000	2.2

BASIC BAKING EQUIPMENT

I am a kitchen tool nerd and have tried almost everything on the market! I've provided a list of what I think constitutes the perfect basic kitchen setup. If you have these tools on hand it will be easy to prepare all the recipes in this book.

Note: Make sure you invest in good-quality kitchen equipment and tools. If you take good care of them, they will last a lifetime.

I have a variety of cake pans in very different price ranges; I find that aluminum cake pans give the best results, as they transfer heat evenly and easily and bake the cake to perfection. The downside to these is that they can't go in the dishwasher.

Here are the basics that I recommend:

Equipment

- Mixing bowls
- Heat-proof rubber spatula
- Metal spatula
- Whisks with metal threads (lots of them)
- Wire rack for cooling the cakes
- Cake tester
- Fine grater
- Grater for root vegetables
- Peeler
- Measuring cups
- Small casserole

Cake Pans

- Small round tin 13 cm (5.1 inch) removable base
- Medium round tin 20 cm (7.8 inch) removable base
- Large round tin 23 cm (9 inch) removable base
- Bread tins in various sizes
- Muffin tray
- Square cake pans
- Small french pie tins, removable base
- Donut hole tin
- Funky shaped tins for special occasions

Machines

- Food processor
- Mini chopper
- Blender
- Stick blender
- Kettle

Miscellaneous

- Baking paper
- Paper cups for baking (various sizes)
- Tin foil
- Cling film
- Paper towels

PANTRY ESSENTIALS

A well-stocked baking pantry holds all the basics for a good cake.
Here is a list of what you will always find in my pantry. I typically have all the dried spices in both ground and whole versions.
However, for baking, stick to the ground spices unless you want to grind them yourself.

SPICES
- Cinnamon
- Nutmeg
- Allspice
- Cloves
- Cardamom
- Dried ginger
- Star anise
- Vanilla
- Black pepper
- Fine salt
- Sea salt

DRIED FRUITS
- Medjool Dates
- Dried figs
- Sultanas
- Raisins
- Cranberries

SWEETENER
- Maple syrup
- Honey
- Date syrup

NUTS AND SEEDS
- Almonds
- Hazelnuts
- Cashews
- Walnuts
- Pecans
- Sunflower seeds
- Pumpkin seeds
- Sesame seeds
- Flax seeds

OILS AND FATS
- Peanut butter
- Almond butter
- Hazelnut butter
- Coconut oil, no flavor
- Neutral flavored oils
- Plant-based "butter" (in the fridge)

FRESH PRODUCE
- Sweet potatoes
- Carrots
- Potatoes
- Lemons
- Limes
- Apples
- Assorted fruits

THE PERFECT DATE

Most of my recipes use dates as a sweetener, which is why I want to spotlight this amazing ingredient. There are many variations of dates, but my favorites are Medjool dates.

The date is a tropical fruit that grows on palm trees (Phoenix dactylifera). It's a small fruit with edible skin and a slim pit in the center. The date originally stems from Morocco, but luckily, it is now grown in warm regions all over the world.

The Medjool dates we buy at the store are dried but not completely dehydrated, giving them their signature texture and flavor, making them easy to work with. You will find many variations of dates, some smaller, some drier, some lighter, and some darker. The darker and drier, the more concentrated the flavor and sweetness will be.

Here's a great tip; if the dates are too dry, you can soak them in boiling water for a few minutes, to soften them up.

A Sugar Alternative

Refined sugar is stripped of minerals, vitamins, and fibers, but dates are a great, delicious, nutrient-dense alternative to sugar in baking. Medjool dates contain about 280–300 Kcal pr. 100 g compare to refined sugar, coming in at 400 Kcal per 100 g.

The Medjool dates I have used weighs about 20 g a piece and is about 12 dates to a cup.

Flavor and Texture

Medjool dates are sweet and have a deep rich caramel-like flavor to them, which adds depth and character to any cake. They are very versatile, and because of their sticky texture, they add creaminess and moisture to the cakes too. But it doesn't stop there; Medjool dates are great to use as a base for icing since they naturally have the right texture and easily absorb flavors to create an abundance of variations of vegan spreads and icings.

Doesn't Spike Your Blood Sugar

Dates are a concentrated source of natural sugars and contain around 66 calories in one date. They are a great source of fiber and contain high levels of essential minerals such as potassium, magnesium, copper, and manganese.

Because of its relatively high content of dietary fiber, the glycemic index of a date is around 53-57 (low/medium GI). This helps slow down the energy release and prevents blood sugar spikes after you eat them, giving you a sustained source of energy throughout your day and on training rides and runs, making the date a perfect date to accompany you on your training and races.

HOW TO FUEL FOR TRAINING

HOW TO FUEL FOR ENDURANCE TRAINING AND RACING

By Dr. Stacy Sims

INTRO

How do you know what to eat and when to eat it? You first need to figure out what works for you. Don't test lots of new things on your most important race day, prepare in advance by testing different options on your medium and longer training sessions.

In the end it comes down to very personal preferences for taste, consistency, and flavor – remember, what works for your best friend or the world champion might not work for you. Before each training session it's a good idea to calculate what, you need, and practice repeatedly in training until you get it right – this way you can be Race-ready and properly fueled on your big day.

TRAINING SESSION OVERVIEW

Short training sessions

Duration: Under 1 hour

Focus: Hydration

Fluid: Plain water with maple syrup and sea salt or a low-carb, electrolyte drink mix.

Fuel: Your glycogen depots should be full from the start of the day and you should be able to perform without eating anything during a 60-minute training session.

It's a good idea to bring a small homemade bar, cake, or a banana, in case your session is extended.

Medium-length training sessions

Duration: 1-3 hours

Focus: Carbohydrate intake

Fluid: 2 bottles of low-carb, electrolyte hydration drinks (depending on the weather, you might need to bring more).

Fuel: 30-60g of carbohydrates from food per hour (about 120-240 Kcal).

Long ride training sessions

Duration: 3+ hours

Focus: Carbohydrate and electrolyte replenishment; food boredom or palate fatigue

Fluid: At least 2-3 bottles low-carb, electrolyte hydration drinks.

Fuel: A total of 30-60g of carbs per hour. Digestion can get harder as rides get longer so eat more solids at the beginning of the ride, switching to blocks, chews, and other easily digested foods during the final part of the ride.

WHAT TO EAT ON A TRAINING PASS?

There are many choices when it comes to picking the right fuel for training. Luckily, this book will give you a lot of options that you can easily adjust to your liking. Let's break it down into categories:

■ Cake (Pick your favorite from the book)
■ Baked bars (Breakaway bar)
■ Rice bars
■ Raw bars (Aerobars)
■ Dried fruit
■ Soft sandwiches
■ Bananas
■ Energy chews (see page 134)

FUELING DURING EXERCISE

You've undoubtedly heard all the carbohydrate recommendations for exercise, with some going up to 80 or 90 grams per hour! It won't surprise you that a lot of these recommendations are calculated for young men. I don't typically recommend specific intakes of carbohydrate grams per hour for either sex, frankly. That said, women do tend to especially benefit from taking in calories from whole foods, which contain a blend of protein, carbs, and fat to fuel their exercise. You're less likely to feel bloated, gassy, and uncomfortably full during long sessions with such mixes of macronutrients than if you keep trying to shovel down more carbs than your gut can process.

A word about gels.

One standard gel packet ranges from 100 to 120 calories per serving. In this there is typically about 33 to 40 grams of carbohydrates, and the recipe is comprised of maltodextrin and fructose with a bit of sodium, potassium, flavorings, and preservatives. If you read the label, you'll see that most product directions state that a gel must be consumed with 2 to 4 ounces of water. That's because gels are very concentrated in carbohydrates. If you don't consume them with an adequate amount of water, they cannot get out of your stomach and into your gut to be absorbed for energy. This means that your body has to pull from its own fluid reserves to water down that gel in order for you to use it, effectively dehydrating you. Gels also contain a blend of carbohydrates that can overload the transport receptors in your gut. This, again, forces your body to pull in water to dilute what is sitting there, leaving you with "goo gut" – bloating, gas, diarrhea, nausea, and general GI discomfort. For the best energy and to avoid GI distress, stick to real food.

TIPS FOR YOUR NEXT LONG ENDURANCE RUN OR RIDE

- Always take more food than you think you will eat, you never know when your body will just need more fuel.
- Plan ahead: know what you will eat and when you will eat it.
- NO BONKING! Don't wait to eat until you get hungry or your energy drops.
- Listen to your body. Learn how it responds to different foods on a ride. We are all a little different so find what is right for you.
- Eat every 30 minutes and double-up midway through a long endurance ride and again in the last 20 miles so you have enough energy to finish well.
- Eat real food that is easy to digest and avoid processed and junk food with high amounts of sugar and corn syrups (such as HFCS).

ABOUT DR. STACY SIMS

Follow Stacy on **drstacysims.com**

@drstacysims

@drstacysims

STACY T. SIMS, MSC, PHD, is a forward-thinking international exercise physiologist and nutrition scientist who aims to revolutionize exercise nutrition and performance for women. She has directed research programs at Stanford, AUT University, and the University of Waikato, focusing on female athlete health and performance and pushing the dogma to improve research on all women. With the unique opportunities Silicon Valley has to offer, during her tenure at Stanford, she had the opportunity to translate earlier research into consumer products and a science-based layperson's book (ROAR) written to explain sex differences in training and nutrition across the lifespan.

Both the consumer products and the book challenged the existing dogma for women in exercise, nutrition, and health. This paradigm shift is the focus of her famous "Women Are Not Small Men" TEDx talk.

Today Stacy lives in New Zealand with her husband, daugther and their dog.

Simple Hydration Drink

500 ml (16.9 fl oz)water
1 tbsp. maple syrup
½ lemon or lime, juice
1/16 tsp. salt

Mix all the ingredients together and cool down.

To learn more about optimal hydration, Scan the code.

BAKING WITH BAKED SWEET POTATO

HOW TO BAKE WITH VEGETABLES

Most of the recipes call for raw vegetables; in these recipes, simply peel the veggies and dice them to a size your food processor can handle. There are a few exceptions where the recipes call for baked sweet potato or pumpkin. Make sure to bake and cool them down in advance.

You will learn how to bake with:

- Sweet potato
- Carrots
- Potatoes
- Beets
- Celeriac
- Pumpkin

SUBSTITUTIONS

If you have parsley root or parsnips, you can substitute those in the recipes that call for carrot, celeriac, and beets. You can also mix and match your root vegetables, playing around with the flavors. If you stick to the correct measurements, it's almost impossible to do anything wrong.

HOW TO BAKE A SWEET POTATO

Bake the sweet potato whole with the skin on at 200ºC/395ºF until the core is completely soft and there is syrup coming out of the bottom of the sweet potato.

Large sweet potatoes (½ kg/1 lb.) will typically take 50-60 minutes to bake, and the smaller ones will take less time.

These can be baked ahead of time. If you plan to make race cakes often, just bake a whole bunch of sweet potatoes, scoop the flesh out, portion out the amount needed for a single recipe into containers, and freeze them.

ABOUT THE SWEET POTATO

My whole cake journey started when I began experimenting with using sweet potatoes as the base for cakes. There are many great reasons they are such an amazing ingredient.

Contrary to what the name suggests, the sweet potato is, believe it or not, not a potato. The sweet potato is not related to the regular potato family (Solanum tuberosum), but a very different family called the morning glory family (Convolvulaceae). The two tubers are not only different in looks, taste, and texture but also slightly different in their nutrient profile. The sweet potato should not be confused with the yam either. Yams are in their own separate family of tubers (genus Dioscorea) and are not like sweet potatoes, they are very starchy and have a neutral flavor.

Nutrition
The nutrient profile of the potato and the sweet potato are quite similar; however, the sweet potato has a significantly higher amount of Vitamin A compared to the regular potato, which only beats the sweet potato with a slightly higher amount of potassium.

	White potato per 100 g/3.5 oz.	Sweet potato per 100 g/3.5 oz
Calories	92	90
Protein	2 grams	2 grams
Fat	0.15 grams	0.15 grams
Carbs	21 grams	21 grams
Fiber	2.1 grams	3.3 grams

VARIETIES

The sweet potato comes in a variety of colors: orange, yellow, white, and purple. Where I live, the most accessible ones are the orange versions and occasionally, I can get hold of the purple ones. They all have slight variations in sweetness, taste, and texture, but most of them can be turned into delicious cakes.

The three most common varieties of sweet potatoes are the Beauregard, The Jewel, and the Garnet. These three types of sweet potatoes are the ones you will find in your grocery store; they are mild in flavor and their flesh is juicy. I will break a few of the different varieties down here:

Beauregard

This is the most common sort of all sweet potatoes; it's larger than the other varieties and has a slightly purple-toned red skin. If you're at your local store and they only have one type of sweet potato, chances are that it's a Beauregard. Bursting with sweetness, a baked Beauregard has a very juicy and slightly stringy texture that works perfectly in these recipes.

Jewel

The Jewel has lighter, orange-colored flesh and is less intense in sweetness compared to the Beauregard. The texture is moist and smooth.

Garnet

The Garnet is easily distinguished from the two other types of sweet potatoes because of its dark orange-red skin. This sweet potato variety is by far the sweetest and moistest of them all, so if you can get your hands on this variety; go for it.

Okinawa

This variety is a purple sweet potato. While it looks absolutely amazing after baking, this sweet potato is a little less sweet than its orange siblings and has a much denser and heavier texture.

Satsuma-Imo

I have spent quite a lot of time in Japan, and the first time I realized sweet potatoes could function as a sweet treat, was on a walk in Tokyo. This variety of sweet potato is served from little food stands, baked with the skin on, and served in tin foil with a napkin on the side, ready to satisfy your sweet tooth and fill you up at the same time. This variety is denser in texture, but still smooth, and it has a slightly sweet and nutty flavor to it. The skin is purple, and the flesh is bright yellow.

The Hannah

Okay, this is funny; there is a variety of sweet potatoes called the Hannah, it's like we were meant to be... or maybe not with this variety. The Hannah has light brown skin and white flesh and is unfortunately not the perfect sweet potato for baking because of its density and low water content. On the flip side, I don't have to cannibalize myself through baking—haha!

Reference: E. Sontag https://www.seriouseats.com/a-field-guide-to-sweet-potato-varieties-and-the-dirt-on-yam

Add protein to any cake

You can add protein to any of the recipes.
I recommend using a high-quality pea protein.
Note, if you add protein to a recipe, you'll need to reduce another dry ingredient or else the cake will be too dry.
Be aware that if you add protein, it's a bad idea to adjust the fat content down at the same time, since the cake will be VERY dry.
If you decide to do this anyway, you should add moisture from, for example, a mashed banana.

Some good extra tips:
You can replace the oatmeal with pea protein, just be aware that it changes the texture and taste of the cake.
Only replace one ingredient at a time when baking, otherwise you won't know what went wrong in the recipe if it turns out dry and weird.
Note all the changes you make and how the result turned out, this way it's easy to remember when you make the same recipe again.

LET'S BAKE

SWEET POTATO RACE CAKES

Yield: 12 cakes, muffin size
Prep time: 10 minutes
Baking time: 25–30 minutes
Equipment: Food processor or blender

Ingredients:

300 g (2 cups) baked sweet potato

4 eggs

65 g (½ cup) rolled oats

2 Tbsp. shredded coconut

6 Medjool dates (120 g)

2 Tbsp. (topped) firm honey (or 3 Tbsp. liquid)

1 tsp. vanilla powder/essence

1 tsp. cinnamon

2 tsp. baking powder

1 lime, zest and juice

½ tsp. salt

100 g (½ cup) melted coconut oil or similar

30 g (¼ cup) blueberries, fresh or frozen

30 g (¼ cup) raspberries, fresh or frozen

shredded coconut for dusting

Tip:

NOTE: You can substitute the berries for
another fruit, such as plums, peaches, or
pears. Be creative!

Make them leaner:

Half the amount of coconut oil.

Process:
Pre-heat the oven to 170°C/340°F

1. Blend all the ingredients except the coconut oil and the berries; blend until smooth.

2. Add in the melted coconut oil while blending at low-medium speed. Taste the batter and season with spices, lime zest, juice, or sweetener if you wish.

3. Grease your muffin tins/paper cups and dust them with shredded coconut.

4. Spoon the batter into the tins/paper cups and press the berries into the batter. If you are bringing them to a race or a training session, make sure to cover the berries completely.

Depending on how tall your race cakes are, the baking time will vary. Try to keep them as flat as possible, about 2.5-3 cm/1 inch.

5. Bake them for 25-30 minutes. If you have a convection oven with a fan, the baking time will be closer to 25 minutes. Otherwise, it will be closer to 30 minutes. Rotate the cakes once during the baking time to ensure even baking. You know your oven best, mine is most aggressive toward the back left corner.

6. The cakes are done when they are golden brown and firm. Cool down and serve right away or wrap them up for your training or that important race day.

SWEET POTATO COCONUT DREAM CAKE

Yield: 1 cake
Prep time: 10 minutes
Baking time: 20 minutes + 10 minutes
Equipment: Blender, cake tin 20 cm (7.8 inch)

Ingredients:

For the cake:

300 g (2 cups) baked sweet potato

1 banana (brown)

4 eggs

45 g (just under ½ cup) rolled oats

7 Medjool dates, pitted (140 g)

4 Tbsp. maple syrup (or honey)

100 ml (3.4 fl oz) almond milk

75 g (¾ cup) unsweetened cocoa powder

1 Tbsp. baking powder

½ tsp. salt

100 g (½ cup) melted coconut oil

Topping:

100 g (1 cup) shredded coconut

3 Tbsp. coconut oil

75 g (¼ cup) maple syrup

½ tsp. salt

Process:
Pre-heat the oven to 170ºC/340ºF

1. Blend all the cake ingredients, except for the coconut oil, until it has a smooth texture.

2. Add the melted coconut oil while blending at low-medium speed.

3. Grease and dust your cake tin with shredded coconut.

4. Pour the batter into the tin.

5. Bake it for 25-30 minutes. If you have a convection oven with a fan, the baking time will be closer to 25 minutes. Otherwise, it will be closer to 30 minutes. Rotate the cake once during the baking time to ensure even baking.

6. Heat all the ingredients for the topping in a casserole and simmer for about 2-3 minutes.

7. Pull the cake out of the oven and spread the hot coconut topping evenly on the top, then bake it for another 10 minutes. Keep an eye on it so it doesn't burn. When the coconut is toasted and golden, it's done.

8. Remove the cake from the oven and let it cool down on a rack. You don't need to wait until it's completely cool; it tastes sooooo good when it's still warm.

TIP: Add chopped nuts to the batter after blending it for a crunchy texture.

This cake will keep for up to five days in the fridge... that is, if you haven't eaten it by day two.
It also freezes well, but the topping might fall off once defrosted. If this happens, you can just put it back on top and slap a dollop of Nice Cream on top and pretend like nothing happened.

SWEET POTATO BANANA BREAD

Yield: 1 loaf
Prep time: 10 minutes
Baking time: 45–50 minutes or until golden brown and firm
Equipment: Blender, bread tin

Ingredients:

300 g (2 cups) baked sweet potato

4 eggs

3 bananas

45 g rolled oats (just under ½ cup) (if your bananas are huge... then add a Tbsp. more)

7 Medjool dates (140 g)

1 tsp. vanilla powder or extract

½ tsp. cinnamon

½ tsp. cardamom

3 tsp. baking powder

½ tsp. salt

100 g (½ cup) melted coconut oil or similar

Optional: shredded coconut for the baking tin

Process:
Preheat the oven to 170ºC/340ºF.

1. Blend all the cake ingredients except for the coconut oil and 1.5 bananas until it has a smooth texture.

2. Add the melted coconut oil while blending at low-medium speed.

3. Grease your bread tin and dust it with oat flour or shredded coconut.

4. Pour the batter into the tin.

5. Peel and cut the remaining 1.5 bananas lengthwise; you can halve them if they are too long. You can essentially cut them however you want since they are for decorating your batter with.
Go bananas (ba dum tss).

6. Bake it for 45-50 minutes until it's firm and golden brown all over. Rotate the bread tin half way through the baking time to ensure even baking. The banana bread is done when it is golden brown, feels firm and sponge and doesn't wobble.

7. Cool down and serve.

It's a lot easier to slice once it's been in the fridge for a couple of hours or even overnight.

Adding protein: You can easily add protein to these race cakes. If you do, I recommend that you substitute about half the oats.

SWEET POTATO RHUBARB CAKE

Yield: 1 cake
Prep time: 10 minutes
Baking time: 40–50 minutes
Equipment: Blender, Cake tin (23-25 cm/9-10in. cake tin)

Ingredients:

300 g (2 cups) baked sweet potato

4 eggs

45 g (Just under ½ cup) rolled oats

6 Medjool dates (120 g)

2 Tbsp. firm honey (or 3 Tbsp. liquid)

1 tsp. vanilla powder or extract

1 tsp. cardamom

2 tsp. baking powder

1 lemon, zest and juice

½ tsp. salt

100 g (½ cup) melted coconut oil or similar

4 stalks of red rhubarb

Process:
Preheat the oven to 170°C/345°F.

1. Blend all the ingredients except the coconut oil and the rhubarb; blend until smooth.

2. Add in the melted coconut oil while blending at low–medium speed. Taste the batter and season with spices, lemon zest, juice, or honey if you wish.

3. Grease your cake tin and dust it with rolled oats.

4. Rinse the rhubarb stalks and cut them diagonally into small pieces or whatever shape you prefer.

5. Pour the batter into the tin and arrange the rhubarb pieces in a creative pattern. Remember it's your time to shine when you serve this cake up!

5. Bake it for 40-50 minutes. If you have a convection oven with a fan, the baking time will be closer to 40 minutes. Otherwise, it will be about 50 minutes. Rotate the cake once or twice during the baking time to ensure even baking.

6. The cake is done when it doesn't wobble, and a toothpick comes out clean when inserted. Cool down and serve.

TIP: You can substitute rhubarb for another fruit, such as cherries, plums, peaches, or pears. Be creative, and when you are, please share it with me online!

BAKING WITH RAW SWEET POTATO

SWEET POTATO CARROT CAKE

Yield: 1 large or 3 smaller cakes
Preparation time: 5 minutes
Baking time: 40–50 minutes, depending on the size of the cake tin
Equipment: Food processor,
Cake tins 1 x 20 cm (7.8 inch)/3 x 12-13 cm (4.5-5 inch)

Cake Ingredients:

200 g (1½ cups) raw sweet potato, diced

2 large eggs

4 Tbsp. honey

2 Tbsp. peanut butter

1 tsp. baking powder

1 Tbsp. vanilla powder or extract

25 g (¼ cup) coconut flour (blend shredded coconut to a fine texture)

30 g (¼ cup) rolled oats

2 tsp. ground cinnamon

2 tsp. ground cardamom

1 tsp. ground dry ginger

½ tsp. ground cloves

2 carrots (120 g/1 cup) peeled and shredded

¼ tsp. salt

Icing Ingredients:

200 g (1 cup) baked sweet potato

1 Tbsp. honey/maple syrup

1 lemon, juice and zest

2 Tbsp. cream (I used plant-based cream)

Process:
Preheat the oven to 175°C/350°F.

1. Wrap the sweet potato for the icing in tin foil and bake it in the bottom of the oven while you make and bake the cake. Bake until completely tender and then cool down before making the icing.

2. In a food processor, process the raw sweet potato into granules. Add the remaining ingredients (without the carrot) and combine well in the food processor.

3. Fold the carrot into the batter.

4. Grease and dust the cake tin of your choice. I used 3 small pie tins approximately 12-13 cm/4.5-5 in. each. You can use a larger cake tin; just remember, the higher the batter is in the cake tin, the longer it will need to bake.

5. Pour the batter into the cake tin(s).

6. Bake on the center rack for about 45-50 minutes, depending on the thickness of the cake. Use a cake tester to check if it's done; when the cake tester comes out clean, you're good.

7. Let the cake cool for a minimum of 30 minutes while making the icing.

8. For the icing, blend the baked sweet potato with the honey, lemon zest, and cream, and then season it to taste with the juice.

9. Top the cake with the icing and serve with fresh and dried berries.

THE SWEET POTATO AMERICAN APPLE PIE

Yield: 1 large cake or 3 smaller cakes
Preparation time: 10 minutes
Baking time: For the large tin, 40-50 minutes; for the small ones, 35-40 minutes.
Equipment: Food processor,
cake tins cake tins 1 x 20 cm (7.8 inch)/3 x 12-13 cm (4.5-5 inch)

Cake Ingredients:

200 g (1½ cups) raw sweet potato, diced

2 large eggs

4 Tbsp. honey

2 Tbsp. peanut butter

1 tsp. baking powder

1 Tbsp. vanilla powder or extract

25 g (¼ cup) coconut flour (blend shredded coconut to a fine texture)

30 g (¼ cup) rolled oats

2 tsp. ground cinnamon

½ tsp. ground cloves

1 large apple, diced

2 Tbsp. coconut sugar (or you can use maple)

1 handful of chopped nuts (optional)

¼ tsp. salt

Process:
Preheat the oven to 175ºC/ 350ºF.

1. In a food processor, process the sweet potato into granules. Add the remaining ingredients (without the apple and coconut sugar) and combine well in the food processor.

2. Dice the apple and toss the pieces in coconut sugar with half a teaspoon of cinnamon..

3. Grease and dust the cake tin of your choice. I used 3 small pie tins, approximately 12–13 cm/4.5–5 in. each. You can use a larger cake tin; just remember, the higher the batter is in the cake tin, the longer it will need to bake.

4. First, spread the batter in an even layer in the tin(s), then spread out the apples and top with a layer of batter. Alternatively, you can fill the cake tin with all the batter and gently press the apples into the mixture.

5. Bake for 45-55 minutes, depending on how thick your cakes are. A toothpick should come out clean after being inserted into the center of the cake.

6. Let the cake cool before serving it up with nice cream.

THE ATHLETE'S PIE

Yield: 1 large cake
Preparation time: 10 minutes
Baking time: For the large tin, 40-50 minutes
Equipment: Food processor, cake tins

Cake Ingredients:

200 g (1½ cups) raw sweet potato, diced

2 large eggs

4 Tbsp. honey

2 Tbsp. peanut butter

1 tsp. baking powder

1 Tbsp. vanilla powder or extract

25 g (¼ cup) coconut flour

(blend shredded coconut to a fine texture)

30 g (¼ cup) rolled oats

2 tsp. ground cinnamon

1 tsp. cardamom

1 large apple, diced

50 g (½ cup) blueberries/black currant, fresh or frozen

2 Tbsp. coconut sugar (you can use cane sugar)

25 g (¼ cup) chopped hazelnuts

¼ tsp. salt

Process:
Preheat the oven to 175ºC/ 350ºF.

1. In a food processor, process the sweet potato into granules. Add the remaining ingredients (without the apple and blueberry and the coconut sugar) and combine well in the food processor.

2. Dice the apple and toss the pieces with the blueberries in the coconut sugar and 1 tsp. cinnamon.

3. Carefully fold the berries and apples into the batter.

4. Line your pie tin with parchment paper and grease it. I have used an American-style pie tin of 21 centimeters, or just over 8 in..

5. Spread the batter into the pan, making sure to even out the surface with a wet spoon or spatula, to prevent any bits from sticking up and burning.

6. Bake for 45-55 minutes until it's golden brown and firm. Test if it's done; a toothpick should come out clean after being inserted into the center of the cake.

7. Cool it down. If you are eating at home with your family and friends, let it cool for a minimum of 30 minutes. If you are bringing it on your ride or run, let it cool down completely in the fridge, so it will be easy to cut and pack.

PODIUM PIE

🅖 🅓 🅢

Ingredients:

200 g (1½ cups) raw sweet potato, diced

2 large eggs

10 Medjool dates (200 g)

2 Tbsp. coconut oil

1 tsp. baking powder

2 tsp. cinnamon

50 g (⅓ cup) pecan nuts

50 g (¼ cup) rolled oats

¼ tsp. salt

3 pears

Process:

Preheat the oven to 175°C/350°F.

1. In a food processor, add all the ingredients (without the pear) and combine well until it's a wet granulate.

2. Cut half the pears into 1 cm (⅜ inch) wedges. Finely dice the rest of the pears.

3. Fold the diced pears into the mixture.

4. Line your pie tin with parchment paper, grease it, and fill it with the batter. Make sure to even out the surface of the batter with a wet spoon or spatula, to prevent any bits from sticking up and burning.

5. Decorate the top with the pear wedges and possibly some more pecans; act like you're a finalist in a baking show, without the stress and the sugar fondant.

6. Bake for 45-55 minutes until it's golden brown and firm; poke it to test the firmness. If your finger breaks through, bake it some more.

7. Cool it down. If you are eating it at home with your family and friends, let it cool for a minimum of 30 minutes. If you are bringing it on your ride or run, let it cool down completely in the fridge, so it will be easier to cut and pack.

Yield: 1 large round cake (20cm/8in).
Preparation time: 5–10 minutes
Baking time: 40–50 minutes, depending on the size of the cake tin
Equipment: Food processor, blender, cake tin

PURPLE PODIUM PIE

G *D* *S*

Yield: 1 large round cake (20cm/8in).
Preparation time: 5–10 minutes
Baking time: 40–50 minutes, depending on the size of the cake tin
Equipment: Food processor, blender, cake tin

Cake Ingredients:

200 g (1½ cups) raw purple sweet potato, diced

2 large eggs

10 Medjool dates, pitted (200 g)

2 Tbsp. coconut oil

1 tsp. baking powder

2 tsp. cardamom

50 g (⅓ cup) cashews

30 g (¼ cup) rolled oats

¼ tsp. salt

2 firm plums

Orange Spread:

12 Medjool dates

(pitted and soaked in a small bowl of boiling water)

1 lemon, juice and zest

1 small orange, juice and zest

4 Tbsp. melted coconut oil

or plant-based "butter"

1 pinch of salt

Process:
Preheat the oven to 175ºC/ 350ºF.

1. In a food processor, add all the cake ingredients (without the plums) and combine well until it's a wet granulate.

2. Cut all the plums into fine dice.

3. Fold the diced plums into the mixture.

4. Grease and dust your cake tin and fill it with the batter; make sure to even out the surface of the batter with a wet spoon or spatula to prevent any bits from sticking up and burning.

5. Bake it for 45–55 minutes until it's golden brown and firm; poke it to test firmness. If it feels too soft, bake it some more.

6. While the cake is baking, make the sweet and tangy orange spread. In a blender, blend the soaked dates without the water, but with the orange juice, zest, and salt until smooth.

7. Add the melted coconut oil while blending at medium speed until it has a smooth texture. Season with lemon juice or salt if needed and adjust the texture with the soaking water.

8. When the Podium pie is done, cool it down before icing it.

LIP-SMACKING LEMON CAKE

Yield: 1 large cake (my cake tin is a 20cm/8.5 in. round)
Preparation time: 10 minutes
Baking time: 40–50 minutes, depending on the size of the cake tin
Equipment: Food processor, blender, cake tin

Ingredients:

200 g (1½ cups) raw sweet potato, diced

2 large eggs

10 Medjool dates, pitted (200 g)

2 Tbsp. coconut oil

1 tsp. baking powder

2 lemons, juice and zest

¼ tsp. salt

50 g (⅓ cup) almonds

30 g (¼ cup) rolled oats

Sweet and Tangy Lemon Spread:

12 Medjool dates, pitted

(pitted and soaked in a small bowl of boiling water)

1–2 lemons, juice and zest

4 Tbsp. melted coconut oil or plant-based "butter"

1 pinch of salt

Process:
Preheat the oven to 175ºC/ 350ºF.

1. In a food processor, add all the cake ingredients and combine well until it's a wet granulate.

2. Grease and dust your cake tin with almond meal, and then fill it with the batter; make sure to even out the surface of the batter with a wet spoon or spatula, to prevent any bits from sticking up and burning.

3. Bake it for 45-55 minutes until it's golden brown and firm; poke it to test firmness. If your finger breaks through, bake it some more.

4. While the cake is baking, make the sweet and tangy lemon spread. In a blender, blend the soaked dates with the orange juice, zest, and salt until smooth, you can add a bit of water here if the date paste is very thick..

5. Add the melted coconut oil while blending at medium speed until it has a smooth texture. Season with lemon juice or salt and if needed, adjust the texture with the soaking water.

6. When the cake is done, cool it down before icing it.

7. Ice the cake with pretty swirls and serve it to your guests. Sit back and wait for the applause.

SWEET POTATO CHOCOLATE FUDGE CAKE

Yield: 1 cake

Preparation time: 10 minutes

Baking time: 40–50 minutes, depending on the size of the cake tin

Equipment: Food processor, blender, cake tin 20cm/8.5 in.

Ingredients:

200 g (1½ cups) sweet potato, raw, diced

2 large eggs

10 Medjool dates, pitted (200 g)

2 Tbsp. coconut oil

1 tsp. baking powder

4 Tbsp. unsweetened cocoa powder

¼ tsp. salt

50 g (⅓ cup) almonds

30 g (¼ cup) rolled oats

Fudgy Chocolate Spread:

12 Medjool dates

(pitted and soaked in a small bowl of boiling water)

2 Tbsp. cocoa powder

60 ml (2 fl oz) espresso

6 Tbsp. melted coconut oil or plant-based "butter"

1 pinch of salt

Process:
Preheat the oven to 175ºC/ 350ºF.

1. In a food processor, add all the cake ingredients and combine well until it's a wet granulate.

2. Grease and dust your baking tin.

3. Fill the tin with the batter. Press it down firmly and smooth the surface with a wet rubber spatula or spoon.

4. Bake for 45-55 minutes until it's golden brown and spongy. Poke it to test for firmness. If it feels spongy and not mushy or wet, it's done. If your finger breaks through, bake it some more.

5. While the cake is baking, make the fudgy chocolate spread. In a blender, blend the soaked dates with the cocoa powder, espresso, and salt until smooth.

6. Add the melted coconut oil while blending. Season with more espresso or salt and if needed, adjust the texture with the soaking water.

7. Let the cake cool down before icing it... or don't; it works great if you put it on while it's warm, but it will melt a bit–you've been warned.
8. Serve and enjoy!

BAKING WITH RAW ROOT VEGGIES

THE ENDURANCE CAKE

Yield: 1 large cake (my cake tin is a 20 cm/7.5 in. round)

Preparation time: 5–10 minutes

Baking time: 45 minutes

Equipment: Food processor, cake tin

Cake Ingredients:

200 g (1½ cups) raw potatoes (fresh potatoes, skin on and washed; old potatoes, peeled)

2 large eggs

Acacia honey* 80 ml (3 fl oz)

2 bananas

2 Tbsp. coconut oil, no flavor

⅔ Tbsp. baking powder

1 lemon, juice and finely grated zest

½ tsp. salt

50 g (⅓ cup) almonds

80 g (¾ cup) rolled oats

Seeds of 1 vanilla pod (or 1 Tbsp. extract)

*You can use any other liquid honey; just be aware that the flavor and color of the honey will change the color and taste of the cake

Process:

Preheat the oven to 175°C/ 350°F.

1. Dice potatoes.

2. In a food processor, add all the ingredients and combine well until it's a wet granulate. Let the batter sit for five minutes, so the oats can soak up the moisture.
Alternative methods:
If you don't have a food processor, dice the potato as small as possible, and use a blender instead. You could also finely grate the potato and combine everything with a stick blender after.

3. Grease and dust your baking tin with oat flour, which is just milled or blended rolled oats. You can also use almond meal.

4. Fill the cake tin with the batter. Press it down firmly and smooth the surface with a wet rubber spatula or spoon.

5. Bake it for 45 minutes until it's golden brown and spongy. Rotate the cake tin a couple of times during baking to ensure an even surface. My oven burns everything in the left corner if I forget to do so.

6. Poke it to test firmness. If it feels spongy and not mushy or wet, it's done. If your finger breaks through it, bake it some more.

7. Let the cake cool down before cutting it.

THE CLIMBER'S CAKE

Yield: 1 medium cake (my cake tin is a 20 cm/ 8.5 in. round)
Preparation time: 5–10 minutes
Baking time: 40–50 minutes, depending on the size of the cake tin
Equipment: Food processor, cake tin

Ingredients:

225 g (1¾ cup) raw peeled carrots, diced

+ extra for decoration

3 large eggs

10 Medjool dates, pitted (200 g)

2 Tbsp. peanut butter

1½ tsp. baking powder

2 tsp. cinnamon

1 pinch of cloves (optional)

2 oranges (1 juiced and zested for the batter)

1 apple, cut into a small dice

¼ tsp. salt

50 g (⅓ cup) sunflower seeds + extra for decoration

30 g (¼ cup) rolled oats

25 g (¼ cup) cranberries + extra for decoration

Process:
Preheat the oven to 175ºC/ 350ºF.

1. In a food processor, add all the ingredients, except the cranberries and apple; combine well.

2. If you haven't already, dice the apple.

3. Stir in the cranberries and apples.

4. Grease and dust your baking tin with sunflower or almond meal.

5. Fill it with the batter. Press it down firmly and smooth the surface with a wet rubber spatula or spoon so nothing burns while baking.

6. Bake it for 40-50 minutes until it's golden brown and spongy. Poke it to test for firmness. If it feels spongy and not mushy or wet, it's done. If not, it needs more baking time.

7. For the decoration like the image, squeeze the juice of the last orange into a bowl. Peel the last carrot and slice it very thinly on a Japanese mandolin; then marinate the slices in the orange juice.

8. Cool down the cake and decorate it by building a carrot "card house" on top.

CAFFEINE KICK CAKES

Yield: 12 pcs.
Prep time: 10 minutes
Baking time: 25 minutes
Equipment: Food processor
Muffin tray, this is important or else they are going to be very flat!
Muffin paper cups, optional, but an extremely good idea

Ingredients:

200 g (1½ cups) raw beets, peeled, and diced

2 large eggs or 3 small

12 Medjool dates, pitted (240 g)

2 Tbsp. coconut oil

2 tsp. baking powder

2 Tbsp. cocoa powder

2 Tbsp. instant coffee

¼ tsp. salt

50 g (⅓ cup) almonds

30 g (¼ cups) rolled oats

Process:
Preheat the oven to 175ºC/ 350ºF.

1. In a food processor, add all the ingredients and combine until it's a wet granulate.

2. Line your muffin tray with paper cups or grease it with coconut oil and sprinkle chopped hazelnuts into it.

3. Fill the tray with the batter. Press it down firmly and smooth the surface with a wet rubber spatula or spoon.

4. Bake them for 25 minutes until they are spongy and smell amazing.

5. Cool them down before trying to get them out of the tin or the paper cups, trust me.

NOTE: If you are not using paper cups, you will need chopped hazelnuts or more chopped almonds.

HOW TO MAKE NUT, SEED AND OAT FLOUR

If you're like me, and you don't want to pay for an overpriced nut meal, luckily you can make it yourself.

Using a food processor or a mini chopper, you can make your own nut meal.

You should use peeled nuts, when possible, because keeping the skin on before pulsing them into flour will change the look of the finished result and give a slightly bitter taste.

ALMOND MEAL:

500 g almonds

1. Add the almonds to the food processor and pulse to a fine consistency.

Be careful you don't over-process them, or you will end up with grainy nut butter instead.

2. Keep the almond meal in an airtight container for up to three months.

Use the same procedure as above with any other nut or seed.

OAT FLOUR:

500 g / 1lb rolled oats

1. Blend the oats as fine as possible.

2. Keep in an airtight container for up to three months.

HOW TO MAKE YOUR OWN NUT AND SEED BUTTER

Making nut butter takes a powerful blender or food processor. Take my word for it; don't use your mini chopper or a supermarket blender—you will only end up with the smell of burnt plastic. Using a blender can make the nut butter super smooth while a food processor will make it chunky.

ALMOND BUTTER:

500 g almonds

1. Add the almonds to your blender or food processor and blend until they have a smooth consistency.

2. Season with salt.

Be careful you don't burn out your machine; give it a break occasionally and let it cool down before blending again. Once you have a smooth paste, you can season with a bit of sea salt.

Keep the nut butter in an airtight container in the fridge for up to a month.

Use the same procedure as above with any other nut or seed.

IMPACT PIE

Yield: 1 medium cake (my cake tin is 20 cm/8.5in.)
Preparation time: 5–10 minutes
Baking time: 45–50 minutes
Equipment: Food processor, cake tin

Ingredients:

225 g (1½ cups) raw peeled celeriac, diced

3 large eggs

10 Medjool dates, pitted (200 g)

2 Tbsp. coconut oil/butter or plant-based "butter"

1.5 tsp. baking powder

1 tsp. cinnamon

2 tsp. vanilla extract or seeds from ½ a vanilla pod

1 lemon, zest for the batter

¼ tsp. salt

50 g (⅓ cup) cashews + extra for decoration

30 g (¼ cup) rolled oats

Optional Icing:

12 Medjool dates, pitted

½ cup boiling water

Vanilla extract to taste

4 Tbsp. of melted coconut oil or vegan block

1 pinch of salt

Lemon to taste

NOTE: If you don't have a food processor, shred or grate the celeriac as fine as humanly possible on a grater, this is a somewhat time consuming process, but will work.

Process:
Preheat the oven to 175ºC/ 350ºF.

1. In a food processor, add all the ingredients and combine well. Once blended or combined, it might look a bit split and watery; that's okay. Just make sure it's somewhat smooth; it should look almost like marzipan.

2. Grease and dust your baking tin.

3. Fill it with the batter. Press it down firmly and smooth the surface with a wet rubber spatula. If you are making muffins or cupcakes, you can use baking paper in small squares made to fit a muffin tin. I added a large scoop of batter to each.

4. Bake for 45-50 minutes until it's golden brown and spongy. The large cake tin will need closer to 55 minutes. Poke it to test for firmness. If it feels spongy and not mushy or wet, it's done. If your finger breaks through it, bake it some more.

5. Optional Icing: If you are not training with this cake, you can ice it! Soak the dates in boiled water for 5 min. Strain the water from the dates and keep it to adjust the texture. In a blender, blend the soaked dates with 2 Tbsp. water, vanilla extract, and salt until smooth. Add the melted coconut oil while blending to get the desired texture. Season with lemon juice or salt if needed.

6. Cool down the cake, ice it, and serve it.

PUMPKIN PODIUM PIE

Yield: 1 medium cake (my cake tin is 20 cm/8.5in.)
Preparation time: 5–10 minutes
Baking time: 45–50 minutes
Equipment: Food processor, cake tin

Cake Ingredients:

225 g (1½ cups) raw diced pumpkin

3 large eggs

10 Medjool dates, pitted (200 g)

2 Tbsp. coconut oil/butter or plant-based "butter"

1.5 tsp. baking powder

2 tsp. pumpkin spice

¼ tsp. salt

50 g (⅓ cup) cashews + extra for decoration

30 g (¼ cup) rolled oats

2 orange, zest and juice of one for the batter

Pumpkin spice mix:

2,5 Tbsp. cinnamon

2 tsp nutmeg

1 tsp cloves

1 tsp ginger

Icing:

12 Medjool dates, pitted

½ cup boiling water

4 Tbsp. melted coconut oil or vegan block

1 pinch of salt

1 orange zest and juice to taste

Process:
Preheat the oven to 170ºC/ 345ºF.

1. In a food processor, add all the ingredients and combine well.
NOTE: If you don't have a food processor, shred or grate the pumpkin as fine as humanly possible on a grater, this is a somewhat time-consuming process, but will work. Once blended or combined, it should look like a wet granulate, make sure it's somewhat smooth; it should look almost like marzipan.

2. Grease and dust your baking tin.

3. Fill it with the batter. Press it down firmly and smooth the surface with a wet rubber spatula. If you are making muffins or cupcakes, you can use baking paper in small squares made to fit a muffin tin. I added a large scoop of batter to each.

4. Bake for 45-50 minutes until it's golden brown and spongy. The large cake tin will need closer to 55 minutes. Poke it to test for firmness. If it feels spongy and not mushy or wet, it's done. If your finger breaks through it, bake it some more.

5. Icing: In a blender, blend the dates with boiling water, orange zest, juice, and salt until smooth. Add the melted coconut oil while blending to get the desired texture, you can add more water if you want it softer. Season with lemon juice and zest or salt if needed.

6. Cool down the cake, ice it, and serve it.

PUMPKIN RACE CAKES

Yield: 12 cakes, muffin size
Prep time: 10 minutes
Baking time: 25–30 minutes
Equipment: Blender, muffin tray, paper cups

Ingredients:

300 g (2 cups) baked pumpkin

4 eggs

65 g (½ cup) rolled oats

2 Tbsp. shredded coconut

6 Medjool dates, pitted (120 g)

2 Tbsp. (topped) of firm honey (or 3 Tbsp. liquid)

1 tsp. vanilla powder/essence

1 tsp. cinnamon

¼ tsp. ground cloves

½ tsp. nutmeg

2 tsp. baking powder

Zest and juice of 1 orange

½ tsp. salt

100 g (½ cup) melted coconut oil

30 g (⅕ cup) blackberries, fresh or frozen

Shredded coconut for dusting

NOTE: You can substitute the berries for another fruit, such as plums, peaches, or pears. Be creative!
Add protein: You can easily add protein to these race cakes. If you do, I recommend that you substitute about half of the oats.

Process:

Preheat the oven to 170ºC/ 340ºF.

1. Blend all the ingredients EXCEPT the coconut oil and the berries, and blend until smooth.

2. Add in the melted coconut oil while blending at low-medium speed. Taste the batter and season with spices, lime zest, juice, or sweetener if you wish.

3. Grease your muffin tins/paper cups and dust them with shredded coconut.

4. Spoon the batter into the tins/paper cups and press the berries into the batter. If you are bringing them to a race or a training session, make sure to cover the berries completely. Depending on how tall your race cakes are, the baking time will vary. Try and keep them as flat as possible, about 2.5-3 cm/1 in.

5. Bake for 25-30 minutes. If you have a convection oven with a fan, the baking time will be closer to 25 minutes. Otherwise, it will be closer to 30 minutes. Rotate the cakes once or twice during the baking time to ensure even baking. The cakes are done when they are golden brown and firm.

6. Cool down and either serve straight away or wrap it for your training or that important race day.

Freeze your race cakes for up to 3 months.

FLAMME ROUGE CAKE

G D S

Yield: 1 large cake (my cake tin is a 20cm/8.5in. round)
Preparation time: 5–10 minutes
Baking time: 40–50 minutes, depending on the size of the cake tin
Equipment: Food processor, cake tin

Cake Ingredients:

100 g (1¼ cup) raw sweet potato,

peeled and diced

100 g (1¼ cup) raw beets, peeled and diced

50 g (¼ cup) fresh or frozen raspberries

2 Tbsp. dehydrated beet juice

(or natural red food coloring)

3 large eggs

12 Medjool dates, pitted (240 g)

2 Tbsp. coconut oil

1 tsp. baking powder

2 lemons (juice of 1, zest of 2)

¼ tsp. salt

50 g (⅓ cup) cashews

30 g (¼ cup) rolled oats

Red Date Icing:

12 pitted Medjool dates

1–2 lemons, juice and zest

100 ml (3.4 fl oz) boiling water

4 Tbsp. melted coconut oil

1 pinch of salt

1 Tbsp. dehydrated beet juice or natural red

food coloring.

Process:
Preheat the oven to 175°C/350°F.

1. In a food processor, add all the ingredients and combine well until it's a wet granulate.

2. Grease and dust your baking tin. Since we aren't using flour, chuck a handful of almond meal into it and rotate the tin until the sides and bottom are covered, and then pour out any extra almond meal.

3. Fill it with the batter. Press it down firmly and smooth the surface with a wet rubber spatula. The wet rubber spatula will even out the top of the cake so that nothing burns while baking.

4. Bake it for 45-55 minutes until it's golden brown and spongy. Poke it to test for firmness. If it feels spongy but not mushy or wet, it's done. If not, bake it some more.

5. While the cake is baking, make the red icing. Strain the water from the dates. In a blender, blend the soaked dates with the dehydrated beet juice/food coloring, lemon juice, zest, and salt until smooth. Add the melted coconut oil while blending to get the desired texture. Season with more lemon juice or salt if needed. You can add one or two tablespoons of boiling water to the mixture to make it smoother.

6. Let the cake cool down before icing it.

BAKING VEGAN CAKES

VEGAN SNICKERS TART

Ⓖ Ⓓ Ⓢ Ⓥ

Yield: 1 cake (I used 25 cm/10 in.), can be cut/broken into 20–30 pieces
Prep time: 15 minutes
Baking time: 15–20 minutes
Cooling time: 1 hour in the freezer before cutting
Equipment: Food processor or mini chopper, cake tin

For the crust:

165 g (1 cup) salted peanuts

50 g (⅓ cup) almonds

35 g (¼ cup) rolled oats

8 Medjool dates (160 g)

2 Tbsp. coconut oil

1 pinch of salt

For the filling:

15 Medjool dates

3 Tbsp. peanut butter

2 Tbsp. unsweetened cocoa

2 Tbsp. coconut oil

1 pinch of salt

2 Tbsp. chopped salted peanuts

Process:
Preheat the oven to 170°C/335°F.

1. Pulse all the ingredients for the crust in a food processor until it has an even, crumbly texture.

2. Press the crust into a cake tin; make sure it is evened out, so it bakes evenly.

3. Bake for about 15-20 minutes until golden and toasted. It is VERY IMPORTANT that you keep an eye on it; the peanuts will burn when you least expect them to.

4. Remove the crust from the oven and let it cool down in the tin on a rack.

5. Combine dates, cocoa powder, and salt in the food processor, and then add peanut butter and melted coconut oil. This might look a bit crumbly and split, don't worry about it.

6. Fill a mug with hot water and drop two tablespoons into it. Now, the filling goes on top of the crust; this will be sticky and a bit tricky, so have patience and use the hot water and the spoons to help you. Place all the filling on top of the crust (still inside the cake tin) use the wet, warm spoons to spread the filling out evenly, dip and change spoons, so the spoon in use is wet and warm all the time and then smooth the surface with it. Sprinkle with chopped salted peanuts and gently press them into the filling.

7. Place the vegan snicker brittle in the freezer and let it set for a minimum of one hour.

8. Carefully flip the brittle out of the tin upside down onto a plate, and then flip it back over to another plate. Cut or break the brittle. Forget about cutting beautiful pieces of this thing. Just embrace the pattern of however it cracks when you try to cut it, people will love it, I promise you.

SWEET POTATO TARTE TATIN

Ingredients:

1 medium-sized sweet potato

60ml (¼ cup) milk

125 g (½ cup) apple sauce/or date puree

100 ml (3.4 fl oz) oil

120 ml (4 fl oz) maple syrup

3 tsp. vanilla extract

225 g (2 cups) almond flour

100 g (¾ cup) potato starch

2 Tbsp. corn starch

2 tsp. baking powder

1 tsp. baking soda

1 tsp. salt

Yield: 1 large or two smaller tarte tatins
Prep time: 15 minutes
Baking time: 45–50 min minutes
Equipment: nonstick pan 2 x 20cm/8 in.
or 1 x 28cm/11 in.

Process:
Preheat the oven to 160ºC/320ºF.

1. Peel and slice the sweet potato into thin slices; use a Japanese mandolin if you have one.

2. Drizzle 2 Tbsp. maple syrup onto the pan and place the sweet potato slices in a nice pattern on top.

3. Mix all the dry ingredients in a mixing bowl.

4. Mix all the wet ingredients in a separate mixing bowl.

5. Combine the wet and dry ingredients.

6. Pour the batter over the sweet potato pattern and bake for 45 minutes until golden brown.

7. When it's done, carefully take it out of the oven, and let it cool for 5-10 minutes

8. Place your flat serving platter on top of the pan, and with a fast and firm grip, flip the pan and platter upside down and let the cake fall onto the serving tray.

You can serve the cake warm or let it cool down completely on the serving platter.

NOTE: Flip while hot, or it will stick to the pan. If it has cooled down too much, you can warm it up a bit in the oven and then flip it out.

Serve with nice cream.
You can make this with apples, carrots, beets, celeriac, pineapple, or any fruit or firm veg that you would like. Play around with it and find your personal favorite. Don't forget to show me your beautiful creation online!

RED DOT MOUNTAIN MUFFINS

The Grand Tour cake selection

Yield: 12 pieces
Prep time: 5 minutes
Baking time: 30–35 minutes
Equipment: Muffin tray and paper cups

Ingredients:

60 ml (2 fl oz) almond milk

150 g (½ cup) apple sauce

100 ml (3.4 fl oz) oil

120 ml (4 fl oz) maple syrup

3 tsp. vanilla extract

225 g (2 cups) almond flour

85 g (¾ cup) potato starch

2 Tbsp. (¼ cup) corn starch

2 tsp. baking powder

1 tsp. baking soda

1 tsp. salt

2 handfuls of fresh berries

(cherries or raspberries)

Process:
Preheat the oven to 160ºC/320ºF.

1. Mix all the dry ingredients in a mixing bowl.

2. Mix all the wet ingredients in a separate mixing bowl.

3. Combine the dry and wet ingredients well.

4. Fill cupcake papers ¾ full and add the berries.

5. Bake for 30-35 min until golden brown.

Keep in the fridge for 3-5 days or in the freezer for up to 3 months.

BLONDE CITRUS CAKE WITH RHUBARB

Yield: 2 small cakes or 1 large
Prep time: 15 minutes
Baking time: 45 minutes
Equipment: Cake tin (2 x 13.5cm/5.3in.or 1 x 20cm/8.5in.)

Ingredients:

60 ml (2 fl oz) almond milk

150 g (½ cup) apple sauce

100 ml (3.4 fl oz) neutral-tasting oil

120 ml (4 fl oz) maple syrup

1 lime, juice and zest

1 lemon, juice and zest

3 tsp. vanilla extract

225 g (2 cups) almond or cashew flour

85 g (¾ cup) potato starch

2 Tbsp. (¼ cup) corn starch

2 tsp. baking powder

1 tsp. baking soda

3 stalks of rhubarb

Process
Preheat the oven to 160°C/320°F.

1. Rinse and slice the rhubarb diagonally into 2.5 cm/1–inch pieces.

2. Mix all the dry ingredients in a bowl.

3. Mix all the wet ingredients with the finely grated lemon and lime zest in a separate bowl.

4. Combine wet and dry ingredients into a smooth batter.

5. Grease and dust your cake tin(s), and then pour in the batter and decorate with the rhubarb slices.

6. Bake for about 45 min until golden brown. The larger cake tin size might need a little longer.

7. Cool down before serving.

THE GREEN SPRINTERS CAKES

The Grand Tour cake selection

Yield: 12 pieces
Prep time: 5 minutes
Baking time: 30–35 minutes
Equipment: Muffin tin and paper cups

Ingredients:

60 ml (2 fl oz) almond milk

150 g (½ cup) apple sauce

100 ml (3.4 fl oz) oil

120 ml (4 fl oz) maple syrup

3 tsp. vanilla extract

225 g (1½ cups) cashew meal

85 g (¾ cup) potato starch

2 Tbsp. corn starch

2 tsp. baking powder

1 tsp. baking soda

1 tsp. salt

1 tsp matcha

Process:

Preheat the oven to 160ºC/320ºF.

1. Mix all the dry ingredients in a mixing bowl.

2. Mix all the wet ingredients in a separate mixing bowl.

3. Combine the dry and wet ingredients well.

4. Fill the cupcake papers ¾ full.

5. Bake for 30-35 min until golden brown.

Keep in the fridge for 3-5 days or in the freezer for up to 3 months.

DATE SYRUP AND PASTE FOR BAKING

🄶 🄳 🅅

If you have an abundance of dates that are too dry lying around at your house, you can make date syrup.

DATE SYRUP

Ingredients:

1 liter (1 quart) water

500 g (1 lb.+ 2 dates) Medjool Dates pitted and roughly chopped

1. Bring the water to a boil, add the dates, simmer for 10 minutes whist skimming off the impurities

2. Remove from the heat, strain off the liquid and reduce it down to 1/3 of the amount at low heat for about 1 hour until you have a syrup,

3. Pour the syrup into scolded jam jars and cool it down at room temperature. Keep it in the fridge for 2-3 weeks.

4. Blend the remaining dates into a paste.

TIP: The date paste can be used instead of apple sauce in the vegan recipes.

BARS AND BITES

THE BREAKAWAY BAR

Yield: 20 squares
Prep time: 25 minutes
Baking time: 30–35 minutes
Equipment: Square baking pan (I used a 24 x 24cm/9.5 x 9.5in.)

For the filling:

12 Medjool dates (240 g)

200 ml (6.8 fl oz) water or espresso

3 Tbsp. unsweetened cocoa powder

1 pinch of salt

For the crust:

120 g (1 cup) oat flour/blended oats

120 g (1 cup) rolled oats

50 g (⅓ cup) hazelnuts

(hazelnut meal if you're not using a food processor)

1 tsp. baking powder

1 ½ tsp. cinnamon

4 Tbsp. coconut oil, melted

1 large (110 g/½ cup) mashed banana

1 pinch of salt

Process:

Preheat your oven to 165°C/330°F.

For the filling:

1. Bring the water to a boil and soak the dates in the water for about 5 minutes.

2. Blend the dates with ⅔ of the water, cocoa powder, and salt until It's smooth. It should be easy to spread and not too sticky—add more water if the dates were dry from the start. Season with salt and adjust with more cocoa if you want a more powerful flavor.

For the crust:

3. Combine all the crust ingredients in a food processor until it has an even texture. If you don't have a food processor, just give it a good massage with your hands—that should do the trick.

4. Line your baking pan with parchment paper and press down ⅔ of the crust mixture evenly. Add the filling and spread it out evenly with a wet rubber spatula.

5. Spread out the remaining ⅓ of the crust mixture on the top of the filling and press it down firmly. It's okay if it doesn't cover the filling completely.

6. Bake the bars for 30-35 minutes until the crust is nice and golden. If you are using a smaller baking pan or one made of glass/ceramics, your baking time will be longer. If you are using a larger tin, your bars might be too fragile, and the baking time will be shorter—aim for the recommended size.

7. Cool it down completely, put it in the fridge and let it set for a minimum of one hour before cutting it. I recommend that the bar sits overnight in the fridge before cutting it—it can be very crumbly on the first day before the moisture has spread out evenly in it. But again, that's your choice… if you need to eat it, nothing can stop you!

8. Wrap them individually and keep them in the fridge for up to five days or keep them in the freezer for up to three months. Then, you can just grab a couple of frozen ones when you head out the door and they will be ready to eat in no time.

TIP: This bar is crumbly, so if you want it to stick together when bringing it on a training ride, add an additional mashed banana to the crust recipe. It will not be crusty, but it will stick together a lot better. The more banana you add, the denser the oat part gets, and you will need to bake it for a bit longer until it's firm. Try it out and tweak the recipe to your needs.

AEROBARS

Yield: 16–20 squares
Prep time: 20 minutes
Equipment: Food processor or mini chopper, small square container

Ingredients:

10 pitted Medjool dates (200 g)

60 g (⅓ cup) raw almonds

60 g (½ cup) raw cashews

55 g (½ cup) pea protein powder

Zest and juice of 1 lime

¼ tsp. salt

Process:

1. In a mini chopper or a food processor, pulse the nuts until they have a granular texture. The finer you pulse it, the smoother the bars will be. If you like a bit of texture, don't make it into nut flour. Set aside ⅓ cup for later.

2. Add the remaining ingredients to the ⅔ cups of nuts already in the processor and process until it has an even, chunky consistency.

3. Line the square container with cling film and press the date-cashew mixture tightly and evenly into the container. I use a similar container on top of it to flatten it. It's important to compress it as much as possible to keep the bar from falling apart.

4. Let the bar sit overnight, or for a couple of hours in the fridge, for the pea protein to absorb the moisture.

5. Cut into desired sized bars and toss them in the chopped nuts to prevent them from sticking together.

6. Wrap individually and keep in the fridge for 5-6 days, or in the freezer for up to three months.

TIP: I personally keep them in the freezer and just grab a few before I head out the door.

Square Salty "Balls"

Yield: I cut 30 squares, but you can cut them however you like
(42 g of protein in the whole portion)
Prep time: 5 minutes
Cooling time: 1 hour in the fridge
Equipment: Mini chopper, container/tray

Ingredients:

130 g (½ cup) peanut butter

5.5 Tbsp. (⅓ cup) maple syrup

55 g (½ cup) pea protein

50 g (just under ½ cup) rolled oats

25 g (¼ cup) shredded coconut

¼ tsp. salt

1 lemon, Zest and juice

Process:

1. If your oats are large and chunky, I recommend pulsing them in a mini chopper into a chunky flour-like texture.

2. Combine all the ingredients in a bowl, and season to taste with salt.

3. Now, you can spend an eternity making balls out of this thing or you can be like me and press them into a container. It's up to you, but I find that the vegan protein crumbles a bit when I try to make balls.

4. If you are making squares, this is how you do it: Press into a cling film wrapped container or tray, and then smack it in the fridge for a minimum of one hour to set.

5. Cut into squares and wrap individually to bring with you.

SPRINTER'S DELIGHT
Fig and almond bars

Preparation time: 5–10 minutes
Yield: 20–24 bars
Equipment: Food processor, square container

Ingredients:

10 dried figs (200 g)

140 g (1 cup) raw almonds

2 Tbsp. raw unsweetened cocoa powder

Pinch of salt

Zest of an orange (Optional, but amazing)

Chopped nuts or freeze dried raspberries

Process:

1. If your figs are not super soft, soak them in boiling water for 20 minutes, strain the water, and then continue with the recipe.

2. In a food processor, pulse the nuts until they have a granular texture. The finer you pulse it, the smoother your bars will be. If you like a bit of texture, don't make it into nut flour.

3. Add the remaining ingredients and process until it has an even consistency.

4. Line the square container with cling film and press the fig and almond mixture tightly and evenly into the container. I use a similar container on top of it to flatten it. It's important to compress it as much as possible to keep the bars from falling apart.

5. Pop the container in the fridge for an hour before cutting it into desired sized bars.

6. Wrap individually and keep in the fridge for 5-6 days or in the freezer for up to three months. I personally keep them in the freezer and just grab a few before I head out the door.

Pimp them up:
Add a few fresh berries to the mix to give them a bit of extra sazz.
If you are adventurous or Danish, add 1 tsp. raw licorice powder to the mix.
TIP: You can also roll the mixture into balls straight away; just skip steps 4 and 5. Once all the mixture has been rolled, put it in the fridge to set.

PELOTON BARS

G D S V

Yield: 16 pieces
Preparation time: 15 minutes
Baking time: 20 minutes
Equipment: Food processor and a square cake pan

22 Medjool dates, pitted (240 g)

100 ml (3.4 fl oz) strong coffee

145 g (½ cup) peanut or almond butter

2 Tbsp. coconut oil

50 g (½ cup) unsweetened cocoa powder

½ tsp. baking powder

¼ tsp. salt

Optional:

75 g (½ cup) chopped pecans

50 g (⅓ cup) chopped dark chocolate

Process:

Preheat the oven to 175°C/350°F.

1. In the food processor, blend the dates with the coffee until it has a smooth consistency.

2. Add the peanut butter, melted coconut oil, salt, baking powder, and cocoa powder and pulse until combined. If you are adding chocolate and nuts, pulse these in now. You don't want to keep the food processor running—just use the pulse function to make sure you still have some chunks of nuts and chocolate left in there.

3. Cover your baking pan with baking paper and spread out the batter evenly. Use a wet rubber spatula to smooth out the surface.

4. Bake for 20 minutes.

5. Cool down completely, preferably in the fridge, before cutting it into squares. Flip the bars in almond meal if you plan on taking them on rides or dust with coconut powder, if you plan to serve them for you family.

This recipe will keep in the fridge for 4-5 days and in the freezer for up to three months.

BROWN BANANA AND OTHER CAKES

Hannah Banana Bread

Yield: 1 loaf
Preparation time: 10 min
Baking time: approx. 50 min
Equipment: Bread tin (28 x 15 x 7 cm)

Ingredients:

4 bananas (one for decoration)

5 Medjool dates, pitted and chopped (100 g)

2 eggs

100 ml (3.4 fl oz) almond milk

60 g (¼ cup) maple syrup

3 Tbsp. melted coconut oil or plant-based "butter"

¼ tsp. salt

140 g (⅚ cup) fine cornmeal

100 g (1 cup) almond meal

1 tsp. baking soda

1 tsp. baking powder

50 g (⅓ cup) dark chocolate, chopped

Process:
Preheat the oven to 165°C/330°F.

1. Mash the three bananas and the pitted and chopped Medjool dates with a whisk or a fork. Whisk in the eggs, almond milk, and maple syrup.

2. In a separate bowl combine all the dry ingredients except the chocolate.

3. Combine the wet and the dry mixtures until there are no dry lumps in the batter.

4. Dust your bread tin and pour in the batter.

5. Add the chocolate to the top of the batter and push it into the batter with a spoon.

6. Peel and slice the last banana lengthwise, lay it on top of the batter, and gently press it down so it's still visible.

7. Bake for about 50 minutes until golden brown and firm.

8. Cool down completely before slicing.

The Brown Banana: A Dark, Spotted Love Story

The brown banana is just perfect for baking; as the banana ripens, it gets sweeter and more flavorful, great for cakes but terrifying for most pro athletes (at least the ones I've worked with).

As soon as a brown spot shows on the yellow skin, the fruit loses its desirability to most people, and during my time as a chef on a cycling team, I've received quite a lot of overripe uneaten brown bananas from the soigneurs, because the riders didn't want to eat them.

Little did they know, they were going to eat them anyway and with great success, by having them transformed into the shape of cake or ice cream.

As the banana browns, it transforms from a starchy fruit into a simple sugar-packed little pouch, and this is exactly what we are after when baking the legendary Hannah Banana Bread.

What should you do with your brown bananas?

Peel and freeze them for later use.

Brown Banana Chocolate Chip Muffins

Yield: 8 large muffins
Prep time: 10 minutes
Baking time: 20–25 min
Equipment: Muffin tray

Ingredients:

2 medium bananas (230 g/1 cup)

2 eggs, or the equivalent of flax eggs

8 Medjool dates,
pitted and chopped finely (160 g)

4 Tbsp. nut butter

¼ tsp. salt

1 tsp. vanilla extract

3 Tbsp. coconut oil/ melted
plant-based butter

200 g (2 cups) hazelnut meal

1 tsp. baking soda

1 tsp. baking powder

50 g (⅓ cup) dark chocolate, chopped (vegan)

50 g (⅓ cup) hazelnuts, chopped

Paper cups for baking

Process:
Preheat the oven to 170ºC/335ºF.

1. Mash the bananas, and then mix in the dates, nut butter, and eggs. Use a whisk to mash the dates into the mixture as much as possible.

2. Add all the dry ingredients except for the chocolate and combine well.

3. Whisk in the oil until completely absorbed.

4. Fold in the chopped chocolate and hazelnuts.

5. Place the paper cups in a muffin tray; divide the batter evenly until each cup is ⅔ full.

6. Bake for about 23 minutes until golden brown and firm.

7. Cool down slightly before eating.

The muffins will keep in the fridge for 3-4 days and in the freezer for up to three months.

TIP: Make it vegan with flax eggs.

CAFÉ STOP COCONUT BITES

Yield: 20 pieces
Preparation time: 15 minutes
Baking time: 6–7 minutes
Equipment: Food processor, double boiler

Ingredients:

10 Medjool dates, pitted (200 g)

2 eggs

4 Tbsp. coconut oil, melted

140 g (1,5 cups) shredded coconut

1 tsp. vanilla extract

¼ tsp. fine salt

Optional: Dark chocolate, melted

Process:

Preheat the oven to 175ºC/345ºF.

1. Combine the dates, eggs, and coconut oil in a food processor and blend well.

2. Add the shredded coconut and salt, and pulse until combined.

3. Shape the mass into 20 little balls and place them on baking paper. Gently flatten them to about 1 cm/0.4 in. thick.

4. Bake for 6-7 minutes until golden brown.

5. Let them cool while melting the dark chocolate in a double boiler. (A double boiler is a casserole with an inch of water in it and a glass or metal bowl placed on top, with a spoon or fork wedged between the casserole and bowl to let the steam out once the water starts to warm up.)

6. Dip the side that was facing down in the baking tray into the chocolate and sprinkle with toasted coconut.

7. Wrap individually and keep in the fridge for 4-5 days or freeze for up to 3 months.

TIP: You can also sandwich two of the cakes with chocolate in the center to avoid a mess if you bring them for a ride or a run.

HANNAH'S BIRTHDAY CAKE

Yield: 1 cake
Prep time: 10 minutes
Baking time: 25–30 minutes
Equipment: food processor or blender, round large cake tin 23 cm

For the cake

20 Medjool dates, pitted (400 g)

5 eggs

50 g (½ cup) hazelnut flour

For the topping

250 ml (8.4 fl oz) whipping cream (I have used plant based)

100 g fresh berries

Process:

Preheat the oven to 170ºC/345ºF.

1. Blend the eggs and dates until the mixture is light yellow and fluffy.

2. Fold in the cashew flour.

3. Grease and dust a round cake tin.

4. Fill the cake tin with the batter and even out the surface with a rubber spatula.

5. Bake for 25-30 minutes until golden brown and spongy. Rotate the cake tin once or twice during the baking time.

6. Cool down completely on a rack before topping with whipped cream and fresh berries.

Yellow Jersey Cake
The Grand Tour cake selection

Yield: 9 cupcakes + 1 small cake or 1 large cake
Prep time: 10 minutes
Baking time: 45–50 minutes

For the cake

100 ml (3.4 fl oz) apple sauce

100 ml (3.4 fl oz) neutral oil

65 ml (2.2 fl oz) maple syrup

80 ml (2.7 fl oz) plant-based yogurt

2 eggs

2 lemons, zest and juice

6 pitted and chopped Medjool dates (120 g)

130 g (¾ cup) fine cornmeal

85 g (⅝ cup) cashew or almond meal

1 tsp baking powder

1 tsp baking sodas

½ tsp. salt

½ tsp. ground turmeric

1 tsp finely minced fresh ginger

50 g (½ cup) pineapple, diced

Process:
Preheat the oven to 170ºC/335ºF.

1. Add all the wet ingredients plus the turmeric and ginger to a blender, add the pitted and chopped dates, and blend until smooth.

2. Combine the rest of the dry ingredients in a mixing bowl and whisk in the liquid from the blender.

3. Fold in the pineapple

4. Divide the batter into 12 paper cups in a muffin tray.

5. Bake the muffins for 25-30 min and the cake for about 40-45 minutes until golden brown and firm. Rotate the tray halfway through the baking time.

NOTE: If you are baking a large cake, please note that the baking time will be slightly extended. If the cake feels soft in the center, bake it some more.

Serve with diced pineapple.

THE CHAMPIONS CHRISTMAS CAKE

Yield: 1 Christmas cake, donut-shaped
Prep time: 15 minutes
Baking time: 45–50 minutes
Equipment: Food processor, cake tin

Ingredients:

200 g (1 ½ cups) raw sweet potato, diced

4 large eggs

10 Medjool dates, pitted (200 g)

4–5 large dried, soft figs (100 g)

2 Tbsp. coconut oil

100 ml (3.4 fl oz) almond milk

1 tsp. baking powder

¼ tsp. salt

50 g (½ cup) pecan nuts

30 g (¼ cup) rolled oats

100 g (1 cup) almond meal

1 lemon, zest and juice

1 orange, zest and juice

2 Tbsp. Christmas spice

200 g (1⅓ cups) of mixed dried fruits:

50 grams or ⅓ cup each of raisins,
cranberries, sultana, currants, or similar

Cashew Icing:

210 g (1½ cups) raw cashews,
unsalted and unroasted,
soaked in cold water overnight

100 ml (3.4 fl oz) maple syrup

120 ml (4 fl oz) almond milk

1 tsp. vanilla extract

Figs and cranberries for decoration

Christmas Spice Mix:

1 Tbsp. ground allspice

1 Tbsp. ground cinnamon

1 tsp. ground ginger

2 Tbsp. ground nutmeg

½ tsp. ground cloves

Process:

Preheat the oven to 170ºC/345ºF.

1. In a food processor, add all the ingredients (without the mixed dried fruits) and combine well until it's a wet granulate.

2. Fold the mixed dried fruits into the mixture.

3. Grease and dust your cake tin and fill it with the batter. Press it down firmly and smooth the surface with a wet rubber spatula.

4. Bake it for 45-55 minutes until it's golden brown and firm. Poke it to test for firmness. If it feels dense, it's done. If your finger breaks through, bake it some more.

5. Cool it down on a rack and prepare the icing.

6. Blend the cashews, milk, and maple syrup to a smooth paste.

7. Decorate the cake with icing, chopped pecans, and cranberries.

MERRY CHRISTMAS!!!

NICE CREAM FOR CAKES

G D S V

Basic Recipe:

450 g (2½ cups) frozen brown bananas

60 ml (2 fl oz) plant-based yogurt

½ tsp. vanilla extract / Vanilla bean

½ lime, zest and juice

Optional: dates or maple syrup to sweeten.

Process:
1. Blend everything to a smooth consistency in a powerful blender or food processor.

2. Season with lime juice and zest.

3. Serve with your favorite cake.

Add spices, cocoa powder, frozen mango, pineapple, chocolate chips, or berries for variations.

ENERGY CHEWS

NOTE: This recipe contains refined sugar for a purpose. These chews are used for long training sessions, 3 hours or more. Read more about what to consume during training on page 038.

Basic Recipe:

250 ml (1 cup) fruit juice of your choice

200 g (1 cup) sugar

½ lemon, juice

½ tsp. fine salt

1,5 tsp. agar agar powder

TIP: You can change the texture of the chews to your liking.

Adjust the amount of agar agar up if you want a more firm texture.

Adjust the agar down, if you want a softer texture.

If your chews have a grainy texture, they have not been boiled long enough. Always look at the agar agar label for product specific guidelines.

Process:

1. Bring everything to a boil, whilst whisking.

2. Turn down the heat and skim of any impurities.

3. Simmer for about 3–4 minutes.

4. Pour the mixture into a container lined with cling film and let it cool down on the counter. Once room temperature the mixture will be firm and you can now cut them and wrap them individually for bringing on rides. Alternatively put the container in the fridge and cool it down for an hour or over night. The chews will be a little more wet when cutting them, if you do it this way.

Store the chews 3–4 days in the fridge or keep them in the freezer for up to 3 months.

SUPPORT THE AUTHOR
Your online engagement counts!

SHARE, SHARE, SHARE.

The Cake Cookbook baking revolution thrives on your active engagement. So, please help me build a community of fellow cake lovers: Spread the word online and offline.

Each time you share a picture featuring the cover of The Cake Cookbook, or one of your cakes with your community, don't forget to tag me. You are helping to spread the word about easy and healthy baking, making it more possible for me to grow my business and create more exciting cake content for you all to enjoy.

HOW CAN YOU HELP?

- Share an image of you holding The Cake Cookbook.
- Recommend The Cake Cookbook to your friends and family.
- Share stories and posts about the cakes you bake and the events at which they are served.
  (Birthday party, race day, cycling club, at the office etc.)
- Share the cakes you make with your friends.
- Engage with me on Instagram and Facebook.
- Join the conversation on my online posts.
- Join me for my online baking events.
- Don't be afraid to ask questions.
- And importantly, don't forget to tag me and enjoy the cake!

HANNAH GRANT

@dailystews   @hannahgrantcooking

THE END

A-Z Recipe INDEX

Cocoa Powder
Breakaway Bar 107
Chocolate Fudge Cake 071
Coconut Dream Cake 051
Peloton Bars 116
Sprinters Delight 112
Vegan Snickers Tart 092

Coffee
Caffeine Kick Cakes 078
Peloton Bars 116
Breakaway Bar 107

Coconut
The Athletes Pie 062
Café Stop Coconut Bites 124
Coconut Dream Cake 051
Pumpkin Race Cakes 086
Race Cakes 048
Sweet Potato American Apple Pie 061
Sweet Potato Banana Bread 052
Sweet Potato Carrot Cake 059
Square Salty "Balls" 111

Cloves
The Champions Christmas Cake 130
Pumpkin Podium Pie 085
Pumpkin Race Cakes 086
Sweet Potato American Apple Pie 061
Sweet Potato Carrot Cake 059

Cornmeal
Yellow Jersey Cake 128
Hannah Banana Bread 118

Cranberries
The Champions Christmas Cake 130
The Climbers Cake 077

Dates
Café Stop Bites 124
Caffeine Kick Cakes 078
Climbers Cake 077
Coconut Dream Cake 051
Flamme Rouge Cake 089
Hannah Banana Bread 118
Hannah's Birthday Cake 126
Impact Pie 082
Peloton Bars 116
Podium Pie 064
Pumpkin Podium Pie 085
Purple Podium Pie 067
Sweet Potato Banana Bread 052
Sweet Potato Race Cakes 048
Sweet Potato Rhubarb Cake 055
The Champions Christmas Cake 130
Vegan Snickers Tart 092
Yellow Jersey Cake 128

Figs
Sprinters Delight 112
The Champions Christmas Cake 130

Ginger
Yellow Jersey Cake 128
Sweet Potato Carrot Cake 059
Pumpkin Podium Pie 085

Hazelnut
The Athletes Pie 062
Breakaway Bar 107
Brown Banana Chocolate Chip Muffins 123
Yellow Jersey Cake 128
Hannah's Birthday Cake 118

Honey
Sweet Potato Rhubarb Cake 055
Sweet Potato Carrot Cake 059
Sweet Potato American Apple Pie 061
Climbers Cake 077
Pumpkin Race Cakes 086

Lemon
Blonde Citrus Cake With Rhubarb 099
Flamme Rouge Cake 089
Impact Pie 082
Lip-Smacking Lemon Cake 068
Purple Podium Pie 067
Square Salty "Balls"
Yellow Jersey Cake 128
Sweet Potato Rhubarb Cake 055
Vegan Salty "Ball" Squares 111

Lime
Aerobars 108
Square Salty "Balls" 111
Sweet Potato Race Cakes 048
Race Cakes 045

Maple Syrup
Blonde Citrus Cake With Rhubarb 099
Coconut Dream Cake 051
Hannah Banana Bread 118
Red Dot Mountain Muffin 097
The Green Sprinters Cakes 100
Square Salty "Balls"V111
Sweet Potato Tarte Tatin 094
Yellow Jersey Cake 128

Orange
Climbers Cake 077
Pumpkin Podium Pie 085
Pumpkin Race Cakes 086
Purple Podium Pie 067
Sprinters Delight 112
The Champions Christmas Cake 130

Pea Protein
Aerobars 108
Square Salty "Balls" 111

Peanut Butter
Brown Banana Chocolate Muffins 123
Climbers Cake 077
Square Salty "Balls" 111
Sweet Potato American Apple Pie 061
Sweet Potato Carrot Cake 059
Vegan Snickers Tart 092

Pear
Podium Pie 064

Pecan Nut
Podium Pie 064
Pumpkin Podium Pie 085
The Champions Christmas Cake 130

Pineapple
Yellow Jersey Cake 128

Plum
Purple Podium Pie 067

Potato
Endurance Cake 074

Pumpkin
Pumpkin Race Cakes 086
Pumpkin Podium Pie 085

Raspberries
Flamme Rouge Cake 089
Sprinters Delight 112

Rhubarb
Sweet Potato Rhubarb Cake 055
Blonde Citrus Cake 099

Root Vegetables
Caffeine Kick Cakes 078
Endurance Pie 074
Impact Pie 082
Podium Pie 064
Sweet Potato American Apple Pie 061
Sweet Potato Banana Bread 052
Sweet Potato Carrot Cake 059
Sweet Potato Chocolate Fudge Cake 071
Sweet Potato Dream Cake 051
Sweet Potato Race Cakes 048
Sweet Potato Rhubarb Cake 055
Sweet Potato Tarte Tatin 094

Turmeric
Yellow Jersey Cake 128

Thank you!

First, thank you to everyone, who baked along with me during the pandemic, without your amazing feedback and support, this book would never have happened.

Secondly, A huge thanks to my family who has eaten the cakes, given me no-filter feedback, and dealt with me and the work that goes into making a book.

Next, thank you to Helmin and Sorgenfri for taking a chance on a very talkative cake baking cycling chef, I am very thankful for this.

As always, a huge thank you to my mentor and advisor Ilya Katsnelson for everything you have helped me with over the years, as well as in this book venture.

Lastly, thank you to everyone who has supported me over the years, buying my books, liking my posts and cooking and baking from my recipes -

Without all of you people, I would not be able to do what I do.

-Hannah

Thank you!